A·Q·U·A·M·A·S·T·E·R

Today's Essential Guide to the

MAR

AQUARIUM

Tim Hayes • Tristan Lougher • Dick Mills

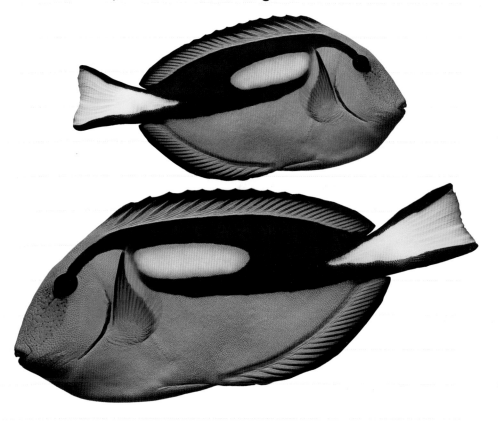

INTERPET PUBLISHING

© 2006 Interpet Publishing
Vincent Lane, Dorking, Surrey,
RH4 3YX, England.
ISBN 10   1 84286 132 8
ISBN 13   978 1 84286 132 5

PUBLISHING CREDITS

Created and compiled: Ideas into Print,
Claydon, Suffolk, IP6 0AB, England.
Design and prepress: Stuart Watkinson,
Ayelands, New Ash Green, DA3 8JW, England.
Computer graphics: Phil Holmes
and Stuart Watkinson.
Principal photography: Geoffrey Rogers
© Interpet Publishing.
Production management:
Consortium, Poslingford,
Suffolk CO10 8RA, England.
Print production: Sino Publishing
House Ltd., Hong Kong.

Printed and bound in China

AUTHORS

Tim Hayes writes extensively on reef aquariums
for aquatic magazines in Europe and the USA.
He lectures on the subject, acts a consultant
and is currently working on a new reef exhibit for
the Blue Planet Aquarium in the UK.

Tristan Lougher is a qualified zoologist with a
passion for marine aquariums. His experience
in the retail side of the ornamental fish industry
enables him to offer vital fishkeeping advice.

Dick Mills' interest in aquarium fishes has lasted
at least 40 years. He still writes for monthly
hobbyist magazines, lectures frequently and has
written many fishkeeping books.

Additional material supplied by Andrew Caine,
Dave Garratt, Steve Halls and Lisa Page.

Below: *The clearfin lionfish* (Pterois
radiata) *is one of the smaller lionfishes
and thus suitable for the marine aquarium.*

Contents

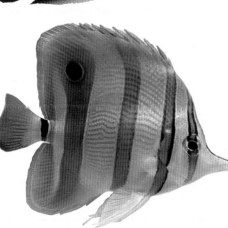

MEETING THE CHALLENGE

Meeting the challenge

If your fishkeeping experience has been confined to tropical freshwater fish, you should consider a number of factors before embarking on the challenge of setting up a marine aquarium. Firstly, bear in mind that the coral reef environment is very stable and marine fish have not evolved mechanisms to deal with unstable conditions in captivity. Secondly, pathogenic organisms do not abound on the reef, so once again, marine fish are ill-equipped to deal with outbreaks of disease in the close confines of the aquarium. You will find that the number of fishes you can keep in a tank of any given size is far fewer than you have been used to and aquarium plants will not feature in the system. Finally, you will need to think about the kind of aquarium you plan to set up: fish-only; live-rock-based fish-only or a reef aquarium. However, if you are prepared to meet the exacting demands placed on the marine fishkeeper, the rewards are well worthwhile.

A FISH-ONLY MARINE SETUP

A fish-only tank will usually contain either larger fish species or those that would prey on invertebrate animals, such as corals, crustaceans, molluscs, etc. Often, aquarists use inert rock for aquascaping due to the perceived likelihood that at some point they will have to use copper-based medications, which are toxic to invertebrates.

*Live rock can be used in a fish-only setup instead of inert rock. Although this precludes the use of copper-based medications, because the live rock is home to large populations of small invertebrate animals, it plays an important part in filtration and provides a healthier environment for fishes, which can browse on it.

LEARN ALL YOU CAN

Investigate all the key issues associated with the hobby, such as maturation of a biological filter; fish and invertebrate compatibility; correct diet and feeding; stocking levels; and the natural behaviour of the species you hope to keep. This vital information will prove invaluable in your marine hobby.

A REEF AQUARIUM

In a reef aquarium, the emphasis is on keeping a display of corals with a few, small, compatible fish, plus sundry non-predatory, mobile invertebrates. Most of the animals found in the marine hobby are collected from different types of coral reef, so it makes sense to research where your fish have come from and then house a selection of animals with the same requirements in terms of water movement, levels of lighting and substrate.

* Decide which animals you want to keep. If the answer is anemonefishes and anemones, the reef design will be quite different from one that would suit small-polyped stony corals, such as Acropora species. This, in turn, will dictate your aquascaping, lighting, water flow requirements, and companion fish and invertebrate species.

▲ *A true skunk anemonefish* (Amphiprion sandaracinos) *nestles inside a bubble anemone* (Entacmaea quadricolor). *The interaction between anemonefishes and their hosts is always attractive to watch.*

◀ *Most fishes and invertebrates are collected from all over the world. A geographically themed reef would be dedicated to fish and invertebrates collected from, say, the Caribbean, the Red Sea, Hawaii, etc.*

Living in a salt solution

The key difference between marine fish and freshwater fish, both coldwater and tropical, is the level of salt found in the water they inhabit, and their ability to survive in that environment. The process by which the salts are absorbed and excreted from the fish's body and the way in which they control their salt levels is known as osmoregulation.

MARINE FISH

Marine fish differ from freshwater fish in the way they balance the levels of salts and fluids in their bodies. The marine environment has a higher salt level than is found in the body fluids of marine fish. As a result, they face a constant battle against dehydration, as water is lost to the surrounding seawater and salts are retained in the body. Marine fish deal with this situation by consuming large amounts of water and excreting very little urine. Only a few salts are absorbed from the seawater they drink; chloride cells in the gills actively excrete salt.

▲ *Marine fishes are well adapted to thrive in a highly salty environment. They can absorb water and excrete the salt to maintain their internal body fluids at the right concentration.*

FRESHWATER FISH

The bodies of freshwater fish contain a higher level of salts than the surrounding water. There is a tendency for salts to be lost through the tissues as water flows in. To combat this, freshwater fish have extremely efficient kidneys that are able to excrete water very quickly while reabsorbing salts from the urine. In addition, their specially structured gills allow them to retain salts circulating in the blood that have been ingested with food.

▲ *A freshwater fish must excrete water constantly so that it does not burst.*

FRESHWATER FISH

Water passes by osmosis from the relatively dilute fresh water into the fish's body.

Salts pass out by diffusion.

The body fluids have a higher salt concentration than the surrounding water.

Kidneys excrete water and retain salts.

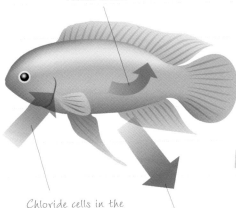

Chloride cells in the gills retain salts from water flowing over them.

Large amounts of very dilute urine.

SALTWATER FISH

Water passes by osmosis from the relatively dilute fish's body out into the sea.

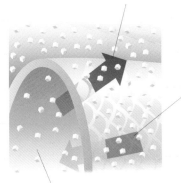

Salts pass in by diffusion.

The body fluids have a lower salt concentration than the surrounding water.

Huge quantities of water are swallowed.

Water, but not salts, are absorbed in the gut.

Salts are actively eliminated by the gills

A small amount of urine is produced.

Choosing and siting a tank

There are various very attractively shaped tank designs on the market, including bow-fronted aquariums. Always choose the largest aquarium you can afford and accommodate. Opt for a tank no less than 90cm long, with a capacity of 136 litres. The larger the tank, the less effect any fluctuations in water conditions will have on marine life. Bear in mind that a tank filled with water and aquarium decor will be extremely heavy and must be placed on a firm base supported on a strong floor. Try to arrange an even distribution of weight across floor joists. Cushion the tank against any unevenness in the stand with a sheet of polystyrene or plastic foam.

▲ Compare the difference in size between a starter freshwater tank (left) and a first marine aquarium.

▼ With a marine tank, especially a reef tank, maximise the breadth (front to back measurement) to reduce the optical foreshortening effect that you get in a water-filled aquarium. The deeper the tank (top to bottom), the more lighting you need. Bear in mind that deep tanks are difficult to service.

* While you are choosing your main display tank, buy another, smaller tank to use as a separate quarantine tank.

▶ Use this formula to calculate the capacity of your aquarium: Length (L) x breadth (B) x depth (D) in centimetres, divided by 1000, gives you the volume in litres. Live rock and other decor will displace the water; reduce the volume by approximately 10 percent to allow for this.

TANK SIZES, CAPACITIES AND WEIGHTS

Tank size (LxBxD)	Volume of water	Weight of water
90x40x38cm	136 litres	136kg
90x45x45cm	182 litres	182kg
100x45x45cm	203 litres	203kg
120x45x45cm	243 litres	243kg
120x60x45cm	324 litres	324kg
150x60x60cm	540 litres	540kg
183x60x60cm	660 litres	660kg

CHOOSING A GOOD LOCATION

Site the tank where it will enjoy stable conditions in a spot away from draughts and vibrations from TV or hi-fi equipment. There must be easy access to an electricity supply. Do not site the tank in direct sunlight or close to a window in a room that receives the midday sun. Adequate ventilation in the room will help to keep temperatures down in summer. Avoid a site close to where toxic fumes, say from a central heating boiler duct, could be drawn back into the tank via an airpump. Site the tank away from regular walkways through the house.

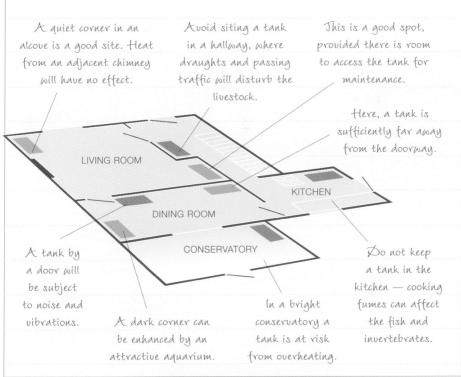

A quiet corner in an alcove is a good site. Heat from an adjacent chimney will have no effect.

Avoid siting a tank in a hallway, where draughts and passing traffic will disturb the livestock.

This is a good spot, provided there is room to access the tank for maintenance.

Here, a tank is sufficiently far away from the doorway.

LIVING ROOM

KITCHEN

DINING ROOM

CONSERVATORY

A tank by a door will be subject to noise and vibrations.

A dark corner can be enhanced by an attractive aquarium.

In a bright conservatory a tank is at risk from overheating.

Do not keep a tank in the kitchen — cooking fumes can affect the fish and invertebrates.

* Leave enough space around the tank for essential maintenance. Keep all the cables neat and tidy and label each one clearly.

◀ *Decide at the outset whether to house all the tank hardware in a fail-safe sump tank beneath the main tank, thus maximising swimming space.*

Aquarium furnishing

In modern marine aquariums, the substrate and rocks play an integral role in maintaining water quality and provide the fishes and invertebrates with a habitat to live in or on. Coral sand and gravel are the most suitable and easily available substrates. Select rocks of calcareous origin such as limestone or coral to avoid the risk of introducing unsuitable materials that may react with saltwater and prove toxic to livestock. Live rock is highly porous and capable of supporting large populations of bacteria, along with small organisms such as algae, crustaceans and molluscs, etc. These animals help to turn the captive reef into a diverse, natural system, while the bacteria process organic wastes produced by the fish and other, larger animals.

◀ *Coral sand and gravel help to maintain a stable pH and high buffering capacity.*

◀ *Ocean rock is suitable for a fish-only setup. Being a dense material, it displaces quite a lot of water.*

LIVE ROCK

Look for rock of low density, preferably pieces showing signs of interesting life, such as tubeworms, calcareous algae, macro-algae, etc. Do not expect to find corals. If you are building a reef on a budget, start with a limited amount of good-quality live rock and then build up the reef with well-cured pieces as you can afford them. The live rock is the infrastructure on which to build up the reef; leave room for adding corals later on. Position the largest pieces at the bottom of the aquarium and work upwards, using incrementally smaller pieces. Leave spaces between them for both the animals and free water movement. Step back to check on your design.

▲ *Live rock, a natural, renewable resource, is mainly composed of coral rubble resulting from storm damage.*

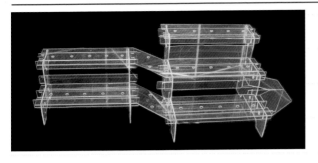

◀ *'Reef racks' slot together to make tiers on which to arrange corals or rocks. In a smaller aquarium you can appear to have substantial rockwork without displacing too much water.*

ARTIFICIAL DECOR FOR A FISH-ONLY SYSTEM

If you are maintaining anemonefishes in a fish-only aquarium, an artificial anemone can help them feel more secure in the company of larger fishes. Imitation corals and sponges provide extra colour. Coral reproductions with an elongate, tree or branchlike structure contrast well with rockwork.

An imitation anemone made of silicone rubber.

An artificial seafan can look surprisingly realistic.

A synthetic stony coral will soon blend in.

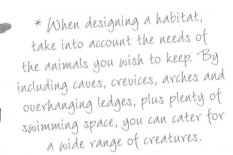

* When designing a habitat, take into account the needs of the animals you wish to keep. By including caves, crevices, arches and overhanging ledges, plus plenty of swimming space, you can cater for a wide range of creatures.

AQUARIUM FURNISHING

Temperature control

The water in a marine aquarium must be maintained at a reasonably constant temperature if fishes and invertebrates from tropical coral reefs are to survive. In a fish-only aquarium, the general guide is to allow 2 watts per litre of water, with the total wattage required being split between two heaterstats where large tanks are concerned. In a reef aquarium of modest size (say 200 litres) heating is required to bring the water up to temperature when you first start off the reef, but subsequently, in the average domestic setting, they will be doing very little work except on the coldest nights. Because of the amount of lighting used above a reef tank to illuminate the corals, it is more likely that you will encounter problems in keeping the temperature below the maximum tolerated by tropical marine organisms.

A heaterstat is a small individual immersion heater combined with a thermostat control.

Use the holder to keep the heating element away from the glass.

A plastic shield protects the base of the glass tube.

▲ A large reef aquarium might not need a heater. While it is lit during the day, heat from the lights is transferred to the water, where it is stored.

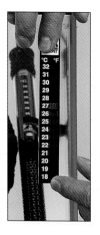

◀ To check water temperatures around the tank, fix a number of external stick-on LCD thermometers at varying depths. Adjust the position of powerheads (water pumps) to eliminate any cold areas.

* As many fish enjoy resting on underwater obstacles, fit a guard over the heater to prevent them from burning themselves. This is essential with slow-moving animals, such as anemones, echinoderms and molluscs.

COOLING THE WATER

Overheating is becoming more and more common, especially with the trend to increased levels of lighting. Installing a cooler is the sophisticated way of dealing with the problem. There are three main designs of cooler: those based on the use of refrigerant gas; on evaporative cooling; and on the peltier element (a thermoelectric system). The last option is the cheapest, but the least efficient and only suitable for smaller tanks.

▶ *Refrigerant coolers are the most expensive option, but highly efficient and easy to plumb in. Some units have additional features; for example, they may also act as a heater or incorporate a built-in UV steriliser.*

◀ *Evaporative coolers are efficient and economical, but you must run an auto top-up system in conjunction with them to deal with the additional evaporation. Vent them outdoors to reduce room humidity.*

▶ *In an emergency, float plastic bags or a food-safe container of ice in the aquarium. Alternatively, freeze the RO (reverse osmosis) water used for topping up evaporation losses and allow it to melt in the tank.*

Lighting the aquarium

Lighting a fish-only aquarium is really down to personal taste. Two fluorescent tubes will usually suffice, with perhaps a third, blue lamp for night viewing. However, if there are invertebrates in the tank, lighting becomes far more important. Many corals, anemones and molluscs rely on microscopic algae known as zooxanthellae for food. As well as good water quality, the main requirement of zooxanthellae is high-intensity light at the correct wavelength. In a reef aquarium, the correct lighting is therefore of paramount importance and this usually means using high-output T5 tubes or metal-halide lamps.

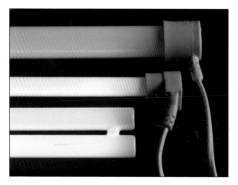

▼ *Actinic tubes give out light that peaks in the blue part of the spectrum. This light is particularly appreciated by invertebrates, including corals. Actinic tubes are often fitted in conjunction with white tubes and switched on before (and switched off after) the white tubes to simulate dawn and dusk lighting. This can also be less stressful for the fish.*

▲ *Traditional T8 fluorescent tubes (top) are 25mm wide and available in various colours. T5 tubes (centre) are 16mm in diameter and provide a brighter light output for their size. These are also available in a compact PL format (bottom) in which the tube is bent back on itself and has four connecting pins at one end of the fitting.*

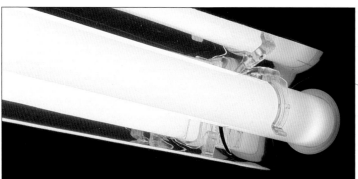

Clip-on reflectors help to maximise the effect of fluorescent light by directing most of it down into the water.

METAL-HALIDE LIGHTING

If unit size or heat output is of little concern, then the light produced by metal halide systems is closest to that experienced by corals in their natural environment. The lamps are defined by the energy they require, e.g. 150- 250- and 400-watt, and by the colour temperature of light that they emit, measured in degrees Kelvin (°K). A 13,000K 150-watt lamp is good for an aquarium up to 60cm deep with a mixture of hard and soft corals. If you wish to keep mostly stony corals in the same aquarium opt for a 250-watt or even 400-watt unit to compensate for the light absorbed by the water.

▲ *Metal-halide lighting units are essential if you plan to keep hard corals, clams and other invertebrates that require high light levels. However, they are costly; if this is a problem consider keeping a fish-only tank until funds are available for metal-halides.*

MAXIMISING YOUR LIGHTING

Light is emitted in all directions. Reflectors direct it into the tank.

Keep condensation trays clean to reduce light absorption.

Particles in the water 'soak up' a large amount of light.

Some light is lost through the glass.

Corals and other invertebrates need to receive high levels of illumination.

◀ *Even well-directed light can be wasted if the cover glass is dirty. Keep everything spotlessly clean.*

* *Some corals can be adversely affected by sudden exposure to more powerful lighting. Suspend a metal-halide unit further above the tank than normal and lower it gradually over several days.*

Water management

The best way of providing suitable water for the marine aquarium is to use an artificial salt mix that is carefully balanced and combined with good-quality tapwater so that the final composition approximates as closely as possible to natural seawater. For the reef aquarium, it is particularly important to make up salt water using fresh water containing as few nutrients as possible. By limiting undesirable nutrients such as phosphates and nitrates from the very start, you have a far better chance of keeping a reef aquarium without constantly battling against pest algae. RO (reverse osmosis) water is a good option. You can treat water by passing it through your own RO unit or buy it from your aquarium dealer, who will fill up a container for you. At the very least, pass domestic tapwater through an aquarium nitrate-removing resin.

* For the reef tank, aim for natural seawater levels of salt, recognised as a salinity of 35ppt (35gm of salt per litre of water).

▶ *A reverse osmosis unit removes contaminants from tapwater.*

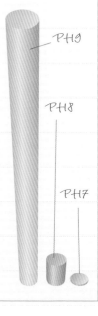

THE pH VALUE

The pH of water is a measure of its acidity or alkalinity. It is measured on a logarithmic scale; 7 is the neutral value. Values below 7 are acidic, while above 7 they are alkaline. Seawater has a higher pH than most fresh water and domestic tapwater and should be maintained at 8.3. A falling pH indicates that the water quality is deteriorating, usually due to an increase in carbon dioxide production because of a build-up of organic debris and because the water's buffering capacities (its ability to resist pH changes) is declining. A 25% water change restores the pH to its normal value. An increase in carbon dioxide (CO_2) levels can also result from insufficient water surface movement or a lack of ventilation.

▶ *Because the pH scale is logarithmic, each unit change is a ten times change. Sudden changes are stressful to fish.*

PH9

PH8

PH7

SPECIFIC GRAVITY AND SALINITY

The terms specific gravity (SG) and salinity can cause confusion. SG (a measure of density) is often used within the marine hobby as a means of assessing the saltiness of the water. However, the correlation between specific gravity and salinity depends on temperature, which means you would get different readings of SG from the same sample of water tested over a range of different temperatures. Salinity is a measure of how much salt is in the water – usually expressed as parts per thousand (ppt) – the same as grams per litre.

▼ A refractometer is another means of measuring salinity. It automatically compensates for temperature and gives a reading in parts per thousand. (An electronic hand-held meter is very accurate but expensive.)

▼ Hydrometers measure the amount of salt in the water in terms of SG. They only give an accurate measurement within a narrow temperature range, which must be appropriate to that of your tank. This is a swing-arm model.

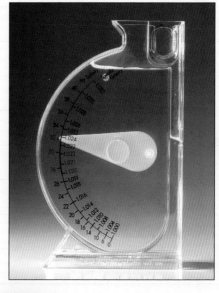

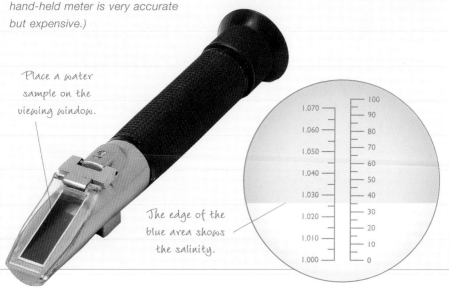

Place a water sample on the viewing window.

The edge of the blue area shows the salinity.

Water management

When setting up an aquarium you can choose between a 'total' or 'customised' system. A 'total system' incorporates integral filters, heating and lighting. It may also include a variety of water management aids, such as a protein skimmer, calcium reactor, UV steriliser and denitrifying unit. The 'customised system' set up on pages 00-00 uses separate pieces of equipment to achieve the three main types of filtration, i.e. biological, mechanical and chemical. It features an externally fitted fluidised bed sand filter for biological filtration, an external protein skimmer for removing organic and chemical waste, and an external power sponge filter to help remove particles in suspension and to improve water movement.

A FLUIDISED BED SAND FILTER

Be aware that fluidised beds and biological filtration in canister filters are unsuitable for the reef aquarium.

◀ A fluidised bed sand filter in a fish-only system has an amazing nitrifying capacity, but the efficiency of the bacteria involved depletes the oxygen content of the water flowing through the unit. Always aerate the water as it returns to the aquarium, either by introducing air into the return tube or using a spraybar to distribute the water over the surface.

A PROTEIN SKIMMER

▶ A protein skimmer removes harmful organic substances from the aquarium before they can cause water quality to deteriorate. In the reaction chamber, a flow of tank water is in close contact with rising columns of air bubbles. Protein waste molecules stick to the bubble surfaces and are carried upwards towards a skimmer cup, where the bubbles collapse, leaving a yellowish liquid that can be removed. Water should be drawn into the skimmer from as near the surface as possible.

AN EXTERNAL POWER FILTER

Plastic tubes carry water to and from the aquarium.

Shut-off taps disconnect the filter without water spillage.

Incoming water passes upwards through the filter media, packed in a plastic basket inside the canister. Maintain water flow at all times to prevent the media turning anaerobic, as would quickly happen following any failure of the power supply.

An electric water pump is housed in the top part of the filter.

A TRICKLE FILTER

If room exists, you can build a simple drip-through trickle filter or tower above the sump in a fish-only system. It is a very efficient form of biological filtration, providing maximum oxygenation and superior nitrification compared to submersed biological filters. Trickle filters cause increased evaporation and consequently heat loss, which can be an advantage or disadvantage depending on the requirements of your system.

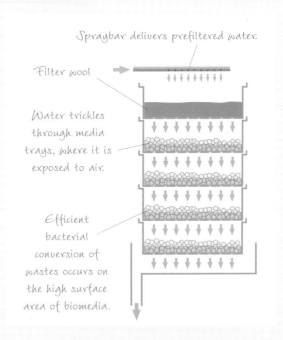

Spraybar delivers prefiltered water.

Filter wool

Water trickles through media trays, where it is exposed to air.

Efficient bacterial conversion of wastes occurs on the high surface area of biomedia.

WATER MANAGEMENT

Water management

Traditional methods of manmade biological filtration are neither advisable nor necessary in a reef aquarium. At the simplest level, all that is needed for a reef aquarium to work is lighting and water flow appropriate to the species being kept. Live rock, mud or deep sand beds (DSB) are the best way of completing the nitrogen cycle in the reef aquarium.

THE BERLIN METHOD

The Berlin method combines protein skimming and the corresponding nitrifying and denitrifying actions of bacteria on the surface and internal interstices of live rock. It is much nearer to a 'natural' method of water management in a reef aquarium compared to earlier methods using manmade biological filtration.

* When using live rock as the basis of a reef aquarium, there is no need to add anything for the maturation process. The bioload of the live rock will take care of that itself.

A DEEP SAND BED (DSB) FILTER

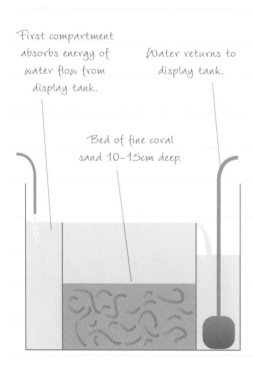

First compartment absorbs energy of water flow from display tank.

Water returns to display tank.

Bed of fine coral sand 10–15cm deep.

◀ *The philosophy behind the deep sand bed (DSB) as used in reef aquariums is very close to that of the Berlin system, but the emphasis here is on a sand bed, 10cm or more deep, to do the natural filtration and denitrification work of live rock. In theory, the vast surface area offered by a DSB will far exceed that offered by a conventional live rock system, allowing you to reduce considerably the volume of tank taken up by rockwork. To work successfully, a DSB must be populated by plenty of small 'creatures', or infauna, various worms and micro-crustaceans, plus meiofauna – predominantly the microbial colonies living on the sand. This is easy to achieve by seeding the bed with a half litre or so of sand from an established reef system.*

THE MUD SYSTEM

The mud system is a natural form of filtration for a reef aquarium that utilises a fine substrate, lit 24 hours a day, where macro-algae in the form of *Caulerpa* are grown. It does not require a protein skimmer or activated carbon to purify the water. It keeps the water well oxygenated through the photosynthesis of the *Caulerpa*, which, being constantly lit, helps to stabilise pH. This method uses the end products of fish metabolism and fixes them into plant tissue, thus preventing the accumulation of ammonia, nitrites, nitrates and phosphates. The *Caulerpa* prevents the growth of undesirable hair algae by competing for essential nutrients; it can be physically harvested to remove nutrients from the system and can also be used as a fresh, natural food for fish.

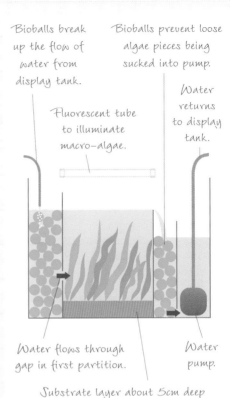

Bioballs break up the flow of water from display tank.

Bioballs prevent loose algae pieces being sucked into pump.

Fluorescent tube to illuminate macro–algae.

Water returns to display tank.

Water flows through gap in first partition.

Water pump.

Substrate layer about 5cm deep supporting growth of macro–algae.

USING CARBON

Carbon will remove the toxic compounds produced by soft corals for the purpose of chemical warfare against rival species, as well as clear up any discoloration of the water. There are three common strategies for using it: either for 24 hours once a month; or for seven days once a month; or use it continuously, replacing it regularly, preferably every six weeks or less. If carbon is used for extended periods it will start to perform as a biological filter, with the risk of elevated nitrates. Even if you do not use it regularly, it is worth keeping some carbon to hand in the event of any emergency where the aquarium water has become polluted. Place the carbon after the mechanical filtration stage so that it does not become clogged.

Setting up an aquarium

First make a list of all the essential items and all the jobs you will need to carry out. It is useful to prepare your saltwater mixture in advance of setting up. If you intend introducing live rock at the setup stage, you cannot make the initial mix directly in the tank. If live rock is to be added a few days later, then it is probably more convenient to mix the saltwater in the aquarium. Make sure that any substrate and rockwork you plan to use in the display are sufficiently cleaned. (This does not apply to the live rock.)

INSTALLING THE TECHNICAL EQUIPMENT

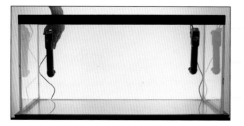

2 Place the return pipe from the external power filter at one end of the tank, where it can be hidden by decor.

1 Place two heaters at opposite ends of the tank for even distribution and to safeguard against heater failure. Elements must not be covered by substrate.

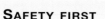

3 Place the inlet filter pipe at the opposite end of the tank from the return pipe for the efficient water circulation.

SAFETY FIRST

- Choose a site for the tank that is near an electric power point and easily accessible, both for setting up and maintenance.
- Leave plenty of space for pieces of equipment around the tank.
- Fit an RCD circuit breaker.
- Do not plug any equipment into the electricity supply until the tank is filled with water.
- Avoid tangling up electrical cables and site connections away from water and splashes.
- Label plugs for future reference.

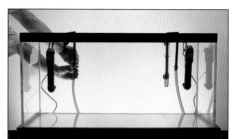

4 Connect hoses to the external power filter. Fit these securely so that they do not come apart when the filter is running under full pressure, otherwise water in the tank will end up on the floor!

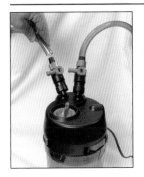

5 Securely connect the hoses to the external filter, without tangling them. It helps to mark them IN and OUT.

6 If you place the aquarium on a cabinet, it is easy to hide away external equipment, such as this external power filter.

7 This protein skimmer hangs on the back panel of the tank. Place it so that the correct operating water level is no lower than that of the aquarium, otherwise it will overflow. Leave easy access for cleaning.

8 This tank incorporates a fluidised bed sand filter. This unit is driven by a small submersible water pump. Attach it inside the tank on the back glass. If possible, site the sand filter and protein skimmer at opposite ends.

9 Hang the fluidised sand bed filter on the outside of the back glass and connect it to the internal pump with a hose. Be sure to fit the chamber containing the sand vertically.

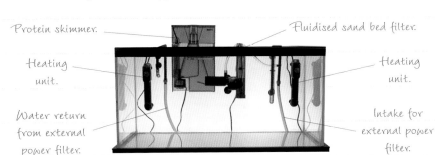

Protein skimmer.

Fluidised sand bed filter.

Heating unit.

Heating unit.

Water return from external power filter.

Intake for external power filter.

Setting up an aquarium

In this setup the decor will serve two purposes: one is to provide cover and territory for the inhabitants and the second is to hide the equipment you have installed. If you cannot afford to create the habitat entirely from live rock, then construct the base features using a cheaper, inert rock. Leave space for any pieces of live rock you propose to add later on. Providing you have a supply of previously matured saltwater to hand that has the correct temperature, specific gravity and pH of 8.3, you can now introduce your pieces of live rock. Add the matured water immediately after placing your rocks and laying the substrate. Work carefully but quickly so that the live rock does not dry out. If you only have newly mixed saltwater available at the setting up stage, wait until the aquarium is fully operational before adding the live rock to avoid damaging the organisms in it.

ADDING THE DECOR

10 Fit a background to the outside of the back glass to hide the equipment. Fish and invertebrate colours stand out well against blue or black.

11 Add the first pieces of live rock directly onto the tank floor. Place them carefully so that you can build up a stable display. In this setup we are using high-quality living rock, with no other form of base rock or other decor.

12 Create a habitat that provides retreats, as well as open swimming space for those fish that require it. Do not allow the live rock to dry out.

13 Spread coral sand around the base of the tank and against the rocks to create a natural effect.

ADDING THE WATER

If you have already matured the water, then it is simply a case of carefully pouring it into the tank. It is a good idea to pour it onto a rock or into a container placed on the substrate to avoid moving the sand out of place.

If you do not have pre-matured water ready, mix a new batch before setting up. Use a spare heaterstat in the mixing container to bring the water temperature up to 24°C so that the salts will dissolve more readily. Once the salts are completely dissolved, take a specific gravity reading. If it is low, add more salts while taking further specific gravity tests until the SG is 1.022-1.023.

▼ *Look out for nitrate and phosphate-free salt mixes and follow the manufacturer's directions exactly. Always use a non-metallic container in which to mix the marine salts with water. Keep a suitable bucket solely for aquarium use. Food-quality plastic buckets are best.*

14 Pour the water gently onto the rocks to avoid displacing the sand. Connect the heating and filtration equipment to the electricity supply and turn it on. Top up the water level if necessary. Monitor the water quality and do not introduce any livestock until ammonia and nitrate levels have been zero for several days.

15 Attach the readout unit of a digital thermometer to the outer glass and place the probe in the water, ideally some distance away from heating units.

Setting up an aquarium

In this setup the lighting canopy is to be fitted with two white 10,000°K fluorescent tubes and one blue actinic 03. You should also be able to cut sections out of the hood to allow filter fittings, hoses and cables to be routed through. A wooden hood laminated with plastic, or painted with several coats of polyurethane varnish, is ideal. Site any control gear for the lamps away from water and splashes. It is worth connecting the power cables for the lights into a remote control box or power strip with the pumps and heaters so that there is only one cable running to the electricity supply socket.

ADDING LIGHTS AND MATURING THE TANK

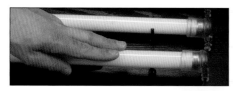

16 Make sure that fluorescent tubes are secured properly into the hood by clips designed for this purpose. Do not use metal clips.

17 Position the tubes in the hood (blue at the back) so they provide the best coverage within the aquarium. Place each tube as far apart as possible from its neighbour to allow for good air circulation, which prevents overheating.

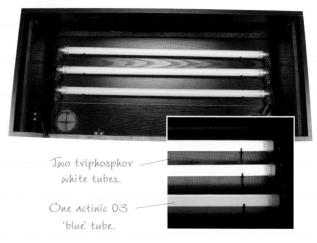

Two triphosphor white tubes.

One actinic 03 'blue' tube.

ALTERNATIVE OPTIONS

The fluidised sand bed filter, protein skimmer and heater units could be fitted into a sump in a cabinet. Fit an overflow from the aquarium to the sump to return water to the aquarium. To improve water movement, install extra pumps, such as small powerheads, in the tank, hiding them behind the habitat. Consider including a UV (ultraviolet light) steriliser to help maintain excellent water clarity and reduced numbers of pathogens.

SETTING UP AN AQUARIUM

MATURING THE FILTERS

Even though there are no animals in the aquarium at this stage, leave the lights on for the normal photoperiod (i.e. 12 hours per day) to help the maturation process. It is essential once live rock has been introduced.

Do not introduce any more livestock into the aquarium until the filters have matured. This means waiting until there is a large enough population of nitrifying bacteria to deal with ammonia and nitrite. The presence of bacteria in the live rock may speed up the process. Make daily tests for ammonia and nitrite levels until readings show zero for both. Levels build up gradually, with ammonia peaking first. Wait until you have had several consecutive days of zero readings before adding livestock. Make a 20-25% saltwater change to dilute the resulting levels of nitrate levels that may form.

▶ *It is vital to understand how the levels of nitrogenous waste products rise and fall during the first few weeks.*

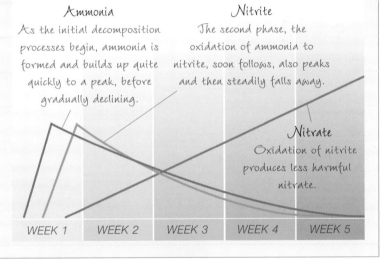

Ammonia
As the initial decomposition processes begin, ammonia is formed and builds up quite quickly to a peak, before gradually declining.

Nitrite
The second phase, the oxidation of ammonia to nitrite, soon follows, also peaks and then steadily falls away.

Nitrate
Oxidation of nitrite produces less harmful nitrate.

WEEK 1   WEEK 2   WEEK 3   WEEK 4   WEEK 5

THE MATURING AQUARIUM

▶ *Monitor water quality before adding any fish. Introducing a 'cleaning gang' of hermit crabs and/or snails controls any developing algae growth while the tank is fish-free and lit for 12 hours a day.*

SETTING UP AN AQUARIUM

Choosing fishes

Several factors must influence your choice of fishes for the aquarium; their compatibility, both with their own kind and unrelated species; their diet; their tolerance of captivity; their appearance and even their cost. Be sure to research thoroughly all the species you would like to keep. Make sure your information is up to date; improvements in factors such as filtration, diet, specimen capture and transport have all made it easier to keep species once considered 'difficult'.

MAKE A LIST

Well in advance of first stocking, make a list of fish species you would like to obtain, now and in the future. Show this to a knowledgeable dealer who can help you minimise territoriality and aggression issues before they arise. Devise a stocking order, starting with the hardier choices and finishing with the most delicate or territorial species.

▲ Examine the fish you intend to buy and observe their breathing rate. Avoid fish that appear to be panting. Do not necessarily ignore a fish with slightly split or damaged fins that is otherwise healthy and feeding. Fins can repair in a few days.

FINS ON A MARINE FISH

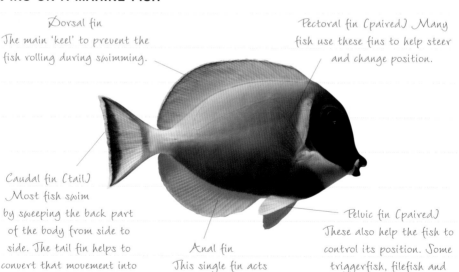

Dorsal fin
The main 'keel' to prevent the fish rolling during swimming.

Pectoral fin (paired) Many fish use these fins to help steer and change position.

Caudal fin (tail)
Most fish swim by sweeping the back part of the body from side to side. The tail fin helps to convert that movement into forward thrust.

Anal fin
This single fin acts as a stabiliser.

Pelvic fin (paired)
These also help the fish to control its position. Some triggerfish, filefish and boxfish lack pelvic fins.

STOCKING LEVELS

As a guide to stocking levels in a reef system, allow 2.5cm of fish per 23 litres of water. In a fish-only system, allow 2.5cm of fish per 11.5 litres. Stick to these levels for the first year of a tank's life. Your chances of success are greatly enhanced if you take a conservative approach while the tank is maturing and stabilising.

▼ *Dealers' fish are always juveniles and most will grow a great deal larger. This polkadot grouper (Chromileptes altivelis) is very appealing as a 5cm juvenile, but less so once it has rapidly grown into a 23cm predator.*

REEF-FRIENDLY FISH

When starting out with a first reef aquarium, choose species of a size proportionate to the size of the tank. For the first year or so, stick to easy-to-keep, small, compatible, reef-friendly fish, such as small planktivores and small herbivores. It is also worth introducing species that undertake a useful role, such as the yellow sailfin tang *(Zebrasoma flavescens)* that grazes many forms of algae.

▼ *In the aquarium, the yellow sailfin tang grazes on algae, including some* Caulerpa *and* Sargassum *species.*

* Build up stocking levels over a period of months. Allow for growth and the final size of the species. Leave room to house a species that you may 'discover' at a later date.

◀ *Not all clownfish require an anemone in the tank. Amphiprion frenatus is an independent species. Others do best when paired with the anemone they associate with in the wild.*

Choosing fishes

The dealer will place your chosen fish in plastic bags filled with one-third aquarium water and two-thirds air, or oxygen if the journey is a long one. Placing these bags into brown paper carriers or coloured plastic bags enables the fish to travel in the dark to help keep them calm. Stow the bags carefully in your car and take the fish straight home.

BAGGING UP A FISH

The dealer transfers your chosen fish into a plastic bag partly filled with water. He then adds oxygen (left) and knots the bag tightly (above). Finally, the fish are placed into dark surroundings (right) for a less stressful journey home.

INTRODUCING THE FISH

1 Equalise the transport water with that in the aquarium by floating the unopened bags in the tank, preferably with the lights off, for about 15 minutes. Then open the bags and roll down the collars.

2 Before releasing the fish, drip some water from the main aquarium into the bag. This avoids adding high-nitrate water (often found in dealers' aquariums) into the home aquarium.

COPING WITH BULLYING

Slightly reorganising the tank decor before adding new fish can help to avoid territorial squabbles, but sometimes a bullying problem occurs after you add a new fish to the tank. The new fish can be either the aggressor or the victim. If the situation does not improve you can try various options. One is to cover the aquarium with a heavy blanket for 48 hours. Theoretically, during this period of enforced darkness, the newcomer will be readily accepted and/or the bully will have calmed down. Another strategy is to place a clear plastic divider in the tank for up to two weeks to separate the dominant bully from the rest of the fish. A further step is to transfer the aggressor to another tank for a week or two to allow the new fish to settle into the display aquarium, but this could stress the bully and disrupt its feeding pattern. Ultimately, you may have to return the bully to the dealer, or if the victim is a single fish, return the victim instead.

*If your aquarium is normally left open, it is a good idea to keep it covered for the first few nights after introducing new fish. Many fish have a tendency to jump at night if they are spooked by other tank inhabitants. Once they have found a refuge they will settle down.

▲ Cowfish are liable to produce a lethal toxin if stressed during transportation. Transport the fish separately (and singly), as any toxin they produce will kill them and everything else in the bag too.

◀ Many popular marine fish are extremely long-lived. Clownfishes can live to be well over 12 years of age and some species of true angel, such as the French angel (Pomacanthus paru) shown left can survive for more than 20 years in captivity.

What are invertebrates?

The term invertebrate loosely covers all those animals that do not have a backbone, or vertebral column, and an internal skeleton. A wide range of invertebrate life can be kept in captivity; suitable species include molluscs, shrimps, crabs, sea anemones, soft and stony corals, starfishes and tubeworms. A piece of live rock may have tiny polyps or fanworms living on it. Many invertebrates coexist with fishes; indeed many fishes and invertebrates have close associations in nature.

INVERTEBRATE HERBIVORES

Invertebrate herbivores help to control problem algae. The usual herbivores to start off with are 'turbo' snails (molluscs) and hermit crabs (crustaceans). 'Turbo' snail describes any of a number of snail species, all with a conical shell. The two most popular hermit crabs are red legs and blue legs. Hermit crabs need a supply of new shells of progressively larger size to move into as they grow.

▲ *Turbo snails are a valuable addition to a reef system. Buy a mix of species, such as* Astraea, Trochus *and* Turbo.

* *Do not be alarmed if you see what looks like the dead body of a hermit crab soon after introduction. It is probably a discarded moult.*

◀ *Hermit crabs can be very entertaining as they try on new shells and return them if they do not 'fit'.*

◀ *Zoanthid yellow polyps are a good first choice of coral, being hardy, colourful and inexpensive. Although it is a photosynthetic coral, it does not depend on really bright light.*

BUYING CORALS

Corals are packed in the same way as fish, although they should be double-bagged to prevent the weight of the rock and water puncturing the bags. In the shop, make sure your coral is bagged under water so that air is not trapped in any areas of the coral, which will lead to the tissue in that area dying. Bagging under water also helps to preserve any sponges that may be attached to the rock.

* 'Frags' are a cheaper way of buying corals. They are fragments of coral that have been fixed to rocks, usually using epoxy glue, and grown on in a coral nursery until they are of marketable size.

▶ *This toadstool coral (Sarcophyton) is one of several soft corals suitable for the marine aquarium. Others include cabbage/finger (Sinularia), colt/pussey (Alcyonium) and cauliflower coral (Cladiella).*

Compatibility

Compatibility is of the utmost importance, particularly when setting up a reef aquarium. The aim is to create a harmonious environment, with none of the inhabitants preying on each other. Compatibility problems are not limited to fish. When invertebrates are added to the mix in a reef aquarium, there is a whole new set of compatibility issues to consider. Many fish will quite happily devour small invertebrates as part of their omnivorous diet. Occasionally the reverse is true; some invertebrates, including mantis shrimps, swimming crabs and *Cerianthus* sea anemones, will prey upon fish. Giant mushroom polyps or large hermit crabs have been known to take unsuspecting fish.

GET ADVICE

If you are in any doubt about compatibility issues with a particular fish, consult your dealer before you buy. Take a list of the fish and other species in your aquarium and ask whether the fish you are considering is a suitable addition.

▼ *The raccoon butterflyfish* (Chaetodon lunula) *eats anemones and polyps. It may even eat smaller ornamental shrimp.*

▼ *Carpet anemones* (Stichodactyla gigantea) *have densely packed tentacles with a powerful sting. They are capable of capturing fish and mobile invertebrates.*

▲ *If a fish is known to exhibit particularly territorial behaviour, such as the humbug aruanus* (Dascyllus aruanus), *introduce it last of all, otherwise it could mercilessly attack any newcomers introduced after it.*

◀ *Compatibility can also mean keeping species together. Some fish team up for foraging purposes. For example, wrasse species (here moon wrasse) often follow triggerfish and parrotfish, which might flush out tiny invertebrates that the smaller fish can eat.*

▶ *If you plan to introduce two closely related and territorial species, such as the yellow sailfin tang* (Zebrasoma flavescens) *and the purple tang* (Z. xanthurum), *first put in a small individual of one species, then a smaller fish of the second species, unless you can add both simultaneously.*

* Tension and aggression will be heightened between fish of a similar size and body shape, or with a similar pattern. The more closely two fish are related, the greater the chance of disputes.

▼ *Bear in mind that there is a difference between invertebrate compatibility and coral compatibility. For example, dottybacks* (Pseudochromis spp.) *will not harm corals, but can present a threat to ornamental shrimp.*

A NATURAL WAR ZONE

Natural reefs are a war zone. Species of coral compete for the available substrate by chemical warfare, overwhelming their 'enemies' through fast growth and by physically stinging them to death. Allow for ample growth when positioning corals.

COMPATIBILITY

The completed aquarium

This is the finished aquarium from the sequence started on page 22, including the initial livestock. Only introduce one fish or invertebrate at a time, unless they are small enough to allow more. Always monitor the water quality before making any further introductions to avoid overburdening the filter system and in turn stressing the animals.

In addition to playing an important role in water quality control, the living rock habitat supports its own community of living organisms, but also provides retreats for other aquarium subjects and a base for adding live corals, anemones and other sessile creatures.

Yellow sailfin tang (Zebrasoma flavescens), a hardy fish ideally suited to this type of aquarium setup.

Skunk cleaner shrimps (Lysmata amboinensis) often perch on rocks advertising their services.

MARINE MACRO-ALGAE

There are many beautiful species of marine algae that, if kept in check, can enhance the appearance of a marine aquarium. However, many are prone to rapid die-off, resulting in the release of a large quantity of nutrients into the aquarium. Regular thinning, rather than occasional heavy pruning, is the best way to keep growth under control. Herbivorous fish such as tangs *(Zebrasoma* spp*)* are useful in controlling macro-algae growth.

▲ Halimeda *sp. is a beautiful alga with a calcareous 'skeleton' that often appears spontaneously from live rock or coral base rock.*

▲ *As its name suggests,* Caulerpa prolifera *grows rapidly under favourable conditions. Harvest it regularly.*

▲ *Grape alga* (Caulerpa racemosa) *has a deserved reputation for accelerated growth followed by rapid die-off.*

◀ *The red alga* Halymenia *sp. is common on live rock and will thrive in nutrient-rich water. Ideal for a beginner's 'algae tank' but it will vanish in tanks poor in nitrate and phosphate.*

A reef aquarium

On these pages we follow the process of setting up a 2.3m-long reef aquarium with a capacity of approximately 1130 litres. It features high-flow water circulation with a large sump (incorporating a deep sand bed), a refugium and high-intensity lighting for optimal coral growth. This sizeable aquarium will accommodate larger fish species, as well as providing space for interesting rockwork architecture.

1 The base cabinet houses the deep sand bed and refugium above it. The cabinet has a steel frame at the back to support the weight of the main tank.

This part of the sump provides a large freshwater top up tank.

2 The main tank was built in situ. The glass base was drilled for water overflow via a weir into the sump and for water returns via closed loops. Very clear, low-iron glass was used for the front and sides.

3 The cabinet houses a protein skimmer (front) and calcium reactor. The skimmer is fed by water from a spur off the main return pump and the reactor by a peristaltic pump from the refugium. Both return water via the sump.

* Asynchronous pumps generate a pulsed water flow to simulate conditions on a typical coral reef.

THE NEXT STAGES IN CONSTRUCTION

4 The main tank was checked for leaks by running the system with tapwater. The closed loop pipes return water at low, middle and high levels for maximal circulation. The overflow weir was placed centrally in the tank in order to collect surface water evenly.

5 The tank was filled with salt water and the sand bed added. The sand was allowed to settle and then the live rock added. During this time the water was heated and recirculated via the main pump with the protein skimmer operational. The system was left to mature in this state for several weeks. Nitrite and nitrate levels were checked regularly during this period to monitor the maturing process.

6 Three sequence pumps are used to circulate the water; one for the main return pump and two for the closed loops. All are fed from the weir. These are located outside in a weatherproof cabinet to reduce noise in the tank room. A hole was therefore made in the wall of the house to accommodate the necessary pipework.

7 Some snails were added one to two weeks after the live rock to control the inevitable algal growth, but also to maintain the necessary beneficial denitrifying bacteria.

* The deep sand bed was added to a depth of 15cm about 2 weeks before the live rock and topdressed with live coral sand.

8 The tank water cleared and signs of life appeared in the rockwork, including tubeworms and microfauna (amphipods, copepods). This confirmed that the tank was maturing properly. The rockwork was arranged into its final position to hide the pipework where possible.

A reef aquarium

9 Corals were added and the main lights switched on. It was important to consider the growth patterns of the corals and their requirements for light and water flow. Corals may attack or shade each other as they grow. The fish were added one at a time with at least one month's interval between additions to minimise the bioburden and stress to the fish. After eleven months there were clear signs of good coral growth.

10 After thirty months, the corals had attained a mature size (particularly the plating *Montipora* coral) and were beginning to encroach on each other. Some careful gardening was required to minimise the corals attacking each other.

* A computer controls and monitors the tank's parameters, including lighting intervals, temperature, pH, conductivity, water flow, water level and calcium reactor.

Compare the size of this blue *Acropora* coral with its growth after a further 19 months — *Step 10*.

11 The frogspawn coral (*Euphyllia* sp.) has grown very large and consists of more than forty individual heads.

12 A large clam sits under the partial shadow of an orange *Montipora* coral. Shadows produced by the spreading corals, such as the blue table *Acropora*, can also provide refuge for fish at night when the lights are switched off.

Feeding

Nutrition has a direct impact on the appearance, colour, growth rate, disease resistance, reproductivity and general well-being of your fish and invertebrates. Their diet must provide the essential components of proteins, fats, carbohydrates, minerals and vitamins. Use a variety of foods to meet these needs. Frozen foods are by far the most popular and appropriate choice for most reef fish. There is a good range available, including foods formulated for difficult feeders, foods enriched with HUFAs (highly unsaturated fatty acids), and foods that have been irradiated to ensure they are parasite-free.

DEFROSTED FROZEN FOODS

Whole cockle
Accepted by many
marine fishes

Marine mix
Natural marine
invertebrate and
fish meats.

Krill
Nutritious food for
larger fish; beak up for
small fishes.

Small fish
A 'one-gulp-food'
for larger fishes

Shrimp
Many wild-caught
foods are irradiated.

* Do not use
fish food aimed at
the freshwater or
coldwater market, as
it may contain too
much fat. Marine
fish need a high-
protein (40-60%)
but relatively low-fat
(5-10%) diet to
thrive.

Frozen foods
are sold in single
slabs. Break off
pieces as required.

Allow frozen
foods to thaw
out before feeding
them to prevent the
fish eating ice.

▼ *Mysis shrimp is a much better 'staple', as it contains a greater percentage of fat and therefore helps to keep weight on fish that might otherwise become emaciated if fed solely on brineshrimp.*

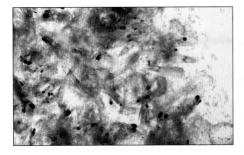

▲ *Brineshrimp is a useful first food for most marine fish, but many species will need far more nourishment than it can provide, even if enriched.*

FLAKE AND GRANULAR FOODS

High-quality mixed flake formulations contain many of the vitamins and proteins required by the majority of marine fish.

Brineshrimp in flake form.

Fast-sinking granular foods help to ensure that bottom-feeding fish receive a supply of food.

DRIED MARINE SEAWEED

Herbivores in the reef should have food available all the time. They need to be constantly browsing. Supplement the algae naturally available in your reef with dried marine seaweeds (macro-algae). You can fit a sheet in a sucker-mounted clip or between the two halves of a magnetic algae scraper. This way the fish know where to find it and it won't drift around the aquarium to be sucked into the filter.

▶ *Many varieties of macro-algae are available, which is just as well as some tangs have the habit of settling on one type to the exclusion of all others.*

Feeding

Provide your fish with a varied diet to prevent them becoming too set in their ways. Although modern prepared foods contain all the necessary nutrients and vitamins, even the slight differences between various manufacturers' mixes will provide an appetising change for them. When buying frozen foods, buy a different type each week to build up a good range, and then feed in rotation.

◀ *Live phytoplankton is non-polluting. The primary users are mainly the minor animals that go on to feed corals and fish by reproducing and providing edible plankton (eggs, sperm and larvae), or by being eaten themselves.*

▲ *Pufferfish and porcupinefish have formidable teeth, fused into a beaklike structure. These grow continuously. Provide hard-shelled foods, such as frozen whole shrimp and cockle in the shell, to enable these fish to keep their teeth short.*

* *Light is food for algae and also for the zooxanthellae harboured by corals. Make sure yo have appropriate levels of light to maintain the animals and plants you wish to keep.*

TARGET FEEDING

A good method of feeding corals is to mix frozen foods of appropriate size with phytoplankton, plus a measure of tank water. Stir this until the frozen food has defrosted and 'target-feed' the corals using a turkey baster. Gently direct a stream of food at individual corals, until you see them capturing it.

◀ *Persuading predators such as this Fumanchu lionfish (Dendrochirus biocellatus) to accept dead foods can be difficult. Buy fish that are feeding well.*

◀ *Feed fish little and often. Net out any food that remains uneaten after two to three minutes. Try to feed in the morning, late afternoon and just before the lights go out. The morning and night feeds are the most important.*

FEEDING

▶ *Unlike fish, sessile invertebrates cannot chase after food and it has to be delivered to them. Turn off filtrations systems for a short period while feeding invertebrates with liquid food, otherwise the filter will 'eat' the food before the inverts do.*

* Before acquiring any fish species, familiarise yourself with their feeding requirements and be sure that you can meet them.

◀ *Ensure that all the fish get their share at feeding time. Stock the aquarium carefully to ensure that voracious feeders are not kept with delicate species. Some fish become more active at night, so make sure that food is available during the hours of darkness for such species.*

Maintaining the aquarium

Biological changes will occur in the aquarium as it matures. However efficient it may be, a filtration system cannot degrade all the waste products generated by the inhabitants. Organic compounds tend to accumulate in the water, as will nitrate in many tanks. A tendency towards a falling pH level is a natural trend, and trace elements become exhausted over time. The simple process of regular (weekly) partial water changes is the solution to many of these problems.

PARTIAL WATER CHANGES

If there are no apparent algae problems, simply siphon out the water into a bucket using a length of 12mm flexible hose. If there is a biofilm on the water surface, scoop it off using a suitable container. If there is an algae problem, try siphoning with a length of airline. This slows down the rate at which you take water from the tank, allowing you time to siphon out the pest algae. Never mix new supplies of saltwater directly in the aquarium – use a food-safe plastic bucket and ideally mix the new water at least 2-3 days before adding it to the aquarium. This will ensure that the salt has fully dissolved. Check the salinity of newly made-up water before adding it to the tank and again 15 minutes after it has been introduced. If the salinity is too high, slowly add RO water, say one litre at a time. If it is too low, mix up a small amount of water at a higher salinity and add that. Occasionally, it may be necessary to top up due to evaporation loss. As only water evaporates, leaving the salts behind, you must use fresh water for topping up.

Direct the water from the tank into a bucket on the ground.

TESTING pH LEVEL

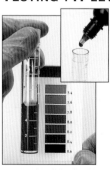

◀ *Check the pH level weekly, making sure it remains stable at around 8.3 – but no higher – and no lower than 8.1. Also take a weekly salinity reading.*

TESTING FOR AMMONIA

◀ *Test ammonia (here) and nitrite levels every two weeks. Both should be zero. It is also a good idea to check nitrate levels; aim for levels below 5mg/litre.*

CLEANING FILTER MEDIA

In a fish-only system, monitor the flow rate of water returning from any external canister filter. If it slows down, the filter needs cleaning. Do not change or rinse out and reuse the entire medium at once. Changing a proportion at a time (using aquarium water to rinse it out) helps to retain the colony of nitrifying bacteria.

▲ *Rinse out filter media in aquarium water to retain the beneficial bacteria.*

◀ *Any build-up of dirt or algae inside the reaction chamber of the protein skimmer (rather than the inside of the collecting cup) may adversely affect the skimmer's efficiency. In a heavily loaded system the protein skimmer may need cleaning once or twice a week. This one is working efficiently.*

* Carry out a daily visual check on the tank. Monitor the behaviour, apparent health and number of your livestock. Check the operation of filters, protein skimmers, powerheads, heaters and airstones. Remove uneaten food or dead livestock.

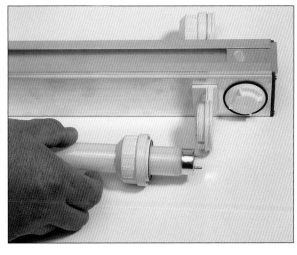

▲ *Change lamps on a regular basis. As a rough guide, replace all fluorescent tubes every 12 months and actinic lamps every six months.*

Maintaining the aquarium

A reef aquarium poses additional maintenance considerations. Calcium can be deposited in such a way as to impair the operation of mechanical equipment. Invertebrates such as snails, sponges and crustaceans can block pipework, leading to flooding and other problems. Clean and service all equipment on a regular basis.

CALCIUM AND CARBONATE

As the number of animals in the reef increases, water changes will no longer be enough to supply their calcium and carbonate demand. For the smaller tank or one with a lower demand, choose one of the balanced, two-part additives on sale. With larger tanks or those with a high demand, it may be more economical to use a calcium reactor or device that automatically mixes kalkwasser. Carbonate and calcium levels are inextricably linked. You can monitor carbonate levels in the knowledge that if these change, it is time to check the calcium levels.

A Counting each drop, add KH reagent a drop at a time to a 5ml sample of tank water. Swirl the tube.
B Initially the sample turns blue.
C As more reagent is added the sample turns yellow. Continue counting the drops added until the yellow colour is stable. Each drop added from the beginning of the test represents 1°dH, equivalent to 17.5mg per litre of carbonate.

A   B   C

A CALCIUM REACTOR

◀ *A calcium reactor passes tank water through a calcareous medium, while adding CO_2 to the reactor. This acidifies the water, dissolving calcium and carbonates in a balanced manner, making them available to the corals.*

✳ *Some salts contain enhanced levels of calcium and carbonate. If your tests show moderately low readings of these minerals, using these mixes may delay the need for supplementation.*

A KALKWASSER STIRRER

◀ *A kalkwasser stirrer mixes calcium hydroxide into RO water, which is then used to top up the tank, thus replenishing calcium while making up for evaporation losses. Calcium hydroxide has a very high pH, which is potentially dangerous to the tank inhabitants as well as humans and other animals. Treat it with care.*

▲ *This 'frag' of Acropora coral needs calcium to develop its stony structure.*

PHOSPHATE TEST

▲ *Add phosphate reagent to a sample of tank water and mix. After five minutes look down the tube to compare the colour of the solution with the chart.*

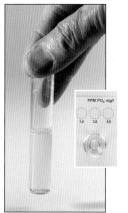

PPM PO₄ mg/l

* *As well as testing for undesirable elements, such as ammonia, nitrite, etc., test kits also tell you what is missing in respect of good components in the water, such as oxygen, iodine and calcium.*

▲ *Regular water testing is vital.*

USING WATER TESTS

Always follow the manufacturer's instructions carefully when testing water parameters; not all test kits use the same technique, especially when it comes to comparing the colours of the test phial against the supplied colour chart. Keep a check on the 'best before' date of the reagents. Liquid reagents age more quickly than dry ones, which can produce misleading results. The shelf life of some reagents is as short as six months, so don't skimp on your testing; make the most of your test kits!

MAINTAINING THE AQUARIUM

Health care

One of the best ways to ensure the good health of your charges, both fish and invertebrates, is to maintain good-quality, stable water conditions, and a stress-free environment. Most health problems usually come down to environmental problems, poor choice of species and equipment failure/malfunction, or aquarist-induced problems, such as inattention, lack of knowledge and 'accidents'. One obvious way to prevent disease is to quarantine all fish and invertebrates before adding them to the display tank.

A QUARANTINE TANK

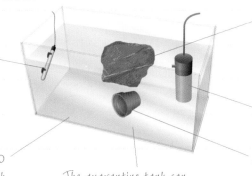

Use a heaterstat to maintain water temperature. Fit a guard to protect fishes that might rest against the heater element.

Slate is an inert material and will not affect the water quality.

Small internal power filter with sponge medium.

Use a small (68–90 litre), clean tank with no substrate.

The quarantine tank can be sparsely furnished.

A clay flowerpot provides a useful hiding place.

WHY QUARANTINE?

Due to the amount of rockwork in a reef system, it is virtually impossible to catch fish established in it. An infected fish can easily pass on disease organisms to other fish, and given the difficulty of treating fish disease in a reef setting, this can quite easily lead to a fish wipe-out. That is why quarantining new fish is so vital. The recommended quarantine period for new fish is usually 14-21 days. Quarantining invertebrates for 7-14 days gives you a chance to avoid introducing potential pest organisms.

▲ It is not possible to treat fishes in the aquarium with copper-based remedies if invertebrates are also present. Although the fish respond well, invertebrates cannot tolerate them at all and will be killed. A few proprietary remedies are safe to use with invertebrates, but these are far less effective than copper. If an infection is severe, it may be best to catch the infected fish and treat it in a separate tank.

▲ *Observe your fish on a regular basis, as the first signs of disease are often seen as behavioural changes. Fish may sulk in the corner of the tank, look 'off-colour' or refuse to feed. Persistent scratching is a sign of irritation, probably parasitic. More obvious signs of disease are ragged fins, inflamed gills and ulceration or spots on the fins, body or gills.*

* If you suspect a problem, first check the aquarium conditions, especially water parameters. Consult reference sources, ask advice and do not rush into inappropriate or unnecessary treatment.

FRESHWATER BATHS

A two- to three-minute freshwater bath can be used as a prophylactic treatment for new fish additions. Any parasites will rupture under the osmotic shock of fresh water long before the fish experiences any harmful effects. The fresh water must be at the same temperature and pH as your tank water. The same treatment can be used to rid corals of predatory nudibranchs and flatworms.

▼ *In the confines of an aquarium, a parasite such as white spot (Cryptocaryon irritans) can complete its life cycle quickly and multiply at a tremendous rate, thus overwhelming the original carrier fish and passing quickly to its tankmates.*

Health care

When using a medication, read the instructions! Some medications may not be suitable for certain fish species. Remove activated carbon media from the filtration system during treatment, as it will remove the medication before a cure is effected. Many medications also require you to suspend protein skimming for the duration of the treatment.

USING MEDICATIONS

If a treatment fails to work, never add another medication straight away. Return the water conditions in the treatment tank to normal before trying another remedy. After successful treatment, always restore the water conditions in the treatment tank to those of the main aquarium before returning the patient.

▼ *Accurate dosing is essential, so it helps to know the exact volume of water in your aquarium. Pre-mix medication in a little tank water before adding it to the treatment tank.*

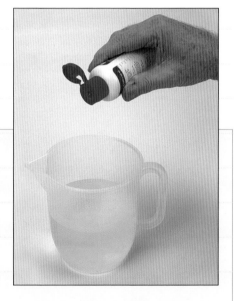

COMMON PROBLEMS

White spot A covering of tiny white spots on the body and fins caused by the parasite *Cryptocaryon irritans*. Treat with copper-based medication.

Velvet Fine white dusting on the skin, giving a velvety appearance. The gills may also be affected. Fish often dash around, breathing rapidly. Caused by *Amyloodinium*. Treat with copper-based medication.

Lymphocystis Fine cauliflowerlike growths on fins and skin. No direct cure. Ozone or UV may reduce spread. May heal on its own in otherwise healthy fish.

Brooklynella hostilis This protozoan parasite causes 'turbidity of the skin'. This is common in anemonefishes and leads to shedding of copious amounts of mucus. The infestation does not respond to copper treatments and is usually associated with poor water conditions, either in the aquarium or during shipping.

UV STERILISATION

UV sterilisation is a very useful, non-invasive way of dealing with a number of diseases, both in the fish-only and reef aquarium. Fish-only systems may well do better with the continuous use of UV sterilisation, taking into account the higher stocking levels. In a sensibly stocked reef system, fish should be at lower risk of stress-induced disease and it is probably sufficient to run UV sterilisation for two to three weeks when adding new fishes. Run the UV when you detect the presence of disease and continue to do so, again for two to three weeks, after the last symptoms of disease have disappeared.

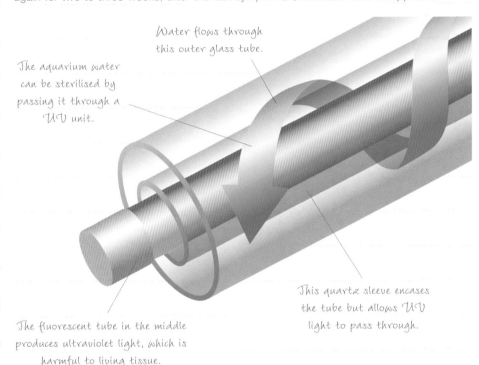

Water flows through this outer glass tube.

The aquarium water can be sterilised by passing it through a UV unit.

This quartz sleeve encases the tube but allows UV light to pass through.

The fluorescent tube in the middle produces ultraviolet light, which is harmful to living tissue.

HEALTH CARE

* Clean and sterilise the treatment tank and all associated equipment after each and every use. To sterilise, either use proprietary aquarium products or those available for treating baby bottles. Rinse well with fresh water and leave to dry.

HUMANE DESPATCH

If all else fails and you have to dispose of a fish humanely, the best option is to obtain the anaesthetic MS222 from a veterinarian. Follow the instructions closely and leave the fish in the solution for a few hours.

Breeding

Breeding marine fish is one of the most rewarding aspects of the hobby and every aquarist should attempt it at least once. Many marine fish will spawn in a reef aquarium. If you are serious about raising the larvae you may have to remove the adult breeding pair to a separate aquarium, where you can observe the potential parents and monitor egg development more easily. The most commonly raised marine fish species are Banggai cardinals and clownfish. Damselfish species, such as gold chromis, neon gobies and various dottyback species also breed readily.

— A juvenile Banggai cardinalfish.

◀ *The female Banggai cardinalfish lays a ball of eggs that the male takes into his mouth for incubation. When they emerge, the young are highly developed and large enough to accept newly hatched brineshrimp and frozen foods of appropriate size. (See also page 61.)*

FEEDING LARVAE

To survive, marine fish larvae first require live foods in the form of rotifers, followed by newly hatched brineshrimp and, finally, dried foods. Feed the rotifers on phytoplankton to keep them alive and reproducing. Keep up the rotifer density and that of the phytoplankton, otherwise the larvae will starve. After five to ten days, depending on species, move on to the brineshrimp, but continue to offer rotifers for the smaller larvae.

Be sure to have food cultures up and running before there are any larvae to raise. Introduce dry foods early on, starting with powdered flake, gradually increasing the food particle size as required. Try feeding new foods first thing in the morning when the larvae are hungry. To avoid the risk of water pollution, be sure to clean out all uneaten food and minimise the amount you introduce until you are sure it is being eaten.

BREEDING

A CLOWNFISH BREEDING TANK

◀ *Clownfishes lay their eggs on a cleaned flat surface. The evening before hatching is due, transfer the eggs to a separate rearing tank, where you can attempt to raise the larvae free of the risk of predation.*

A simple bubble-up sponge filter

Tank measuring 75x30x38cm.

Provide a flat surface, such as a piece of slate, for the fish to lay their eggs on.

An anemone near the slate helps the fish to 'feel at home'.

A LARVAL-RAISING TANK

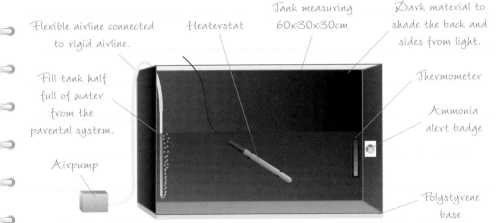

Flexible airline connected to rigid airline.

Heaterstat

Tank measuring 60x30x30cm

Dark material to shade the back and sides from light.

Thermometer

Fill tank half full of water from the parental system.

Ammonia alert badge

Airpump

Polystyrene base

▲ *Set up the larval raising tank as shown here. Prepare a removable black cover for the front glass. Regulate the airflow to provide good water circulation without excessively vigorous bubbling. Ensure that the heater is covered by water. Adjust it over a period of 24 hours to maintain a stable water temperature of 27°C. Provide a photoperiod of 12-16 hours using standard T8 fluorescent lighting.*

* Blacking out the tank makes it easier for the larvae to see their prey and prevents them being distracted by light outside the tank. After five to seven days, when the larvae's eyes have developed a little more, discard the front cover.

Breeding

To encourage any aquatic animal to breed, you must first provide good water quality, followed by a compatible mate, a safe environment and good nutrition. Some species may have further requirements, such as cues that stimulate breeding in the way of, perhaps, the lunar cycle or changes in salinity or temperature, etc. Always find out as much as you can before attempting to breed any marine fish or invertebrate species.

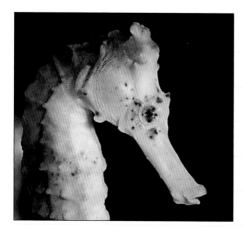

◀ Although the female seahorse produces the eggs, she transfers them to the male's pouch, where they develop until they are ready to emerge as miniature versions of their parents. Captive-bred seahorses often require live brineshrimp to begin with, but can be gradually weaned onto frozen foods, such as chopped mysis shrimp, which is more nutritious.

▶ Most of the invertebrates that reproduce in the aquarium do so by asexual means, whereby the foot of an anemone or polyp splits, producing two daughter colonies from the parent colony. Baby colonies form directly on the stem of soft corals such as Sarcophyton sp.

◀ Two Lysmata shrimps of the same species (here L. amboinensis) constitute a pair. Both will carry eggs on a regular basis, usually releasing larvae late at night. Raise them in a setup as described on page 55. Be sure to prevent the build-up of hair algae in which the tiny shrimps could become caught up. While shrimps are growing and moulting, they remain free-swimming. After the final moult the larvae become true juvenile shrimps and substrate-orientated, only venturing into the water column when food is introduced.

MARINE LIVESTOCK

The sheer variety of suitable marine fish to choose from is one of the main reasons for the hobby's popularity. The most striking tropical marine fishes are native to coral reefs and coastal waters, where collection is quite easy. Fishes from the deepest waters usually grow too large for the aquarium and also present too many collection and transportation problems. The majority of suitable fishes come from the Indo-Pacific Oceans, the Caribbean area of the Northern Atlantic Ocean, and the Red Sea.

When you come to buy your fishes and invertebrates, bear in mind that within every family there are anomalies. Not all species in a particular family may be suitable for aquarium life, so always research your chosen species and seek advice from your aquatic dealer.

When requesting information about a particular species from a dealer, it is helpful to know the scientific (Latin) name to avoid any potential confusion. Certain species will have several common names, but only ever one scientific name. It may seem like a bit of a mouthful, but it could prevent you buying the 'wrong' fish. When buying fish, take accurate information with you about the size of your tank and the existing inhabitants.

On the following pages you will find an introduction to some of the fishes and invertebrates found in each of the families commonly available in aquatic shops. Some are relatively hardy and easy to care for, while others may have specific dietary requirements or behavioural traits   that you must take into consideration before buying.

Many popular marine fish are extremely long-lived, so the choices you make when you first stock your aquarium are very important, as you may well be sharing your living space with these fish for many years to come.

Anemonefishes

Anemonefishes are hardy, relatively inexpensive and readily available. Some are long-lived. They will accept most foods, achieve a modest maximum size and usually tolerate other individuals of the same size. Given good care, they are likely to breed in the aquarium. In common with damselfishes and cardinalfishes, they use invertebrates for protection; in fact, the sight of a common clownfish amongst the tentacles of its host anemone is one that first attracts many fishkeepers to the marine hobby.

◀ *The body colour of Clarke's anemonefish (Amphiprion clarkii) ranges from light brown to jet-black. At 15cm maximum size, females are larger than males (10cm maximum). A large fish can be quite belligerent towards anything that threatens its anemone.*

The fiery coloration of small individuals becomes more subdued with time.

The tomato clownfish can be distinguished from closely related species by the black leading edge of the pelvic fins.

* *Anemonefishes are known to inhabit any one of nine species of host anemone. Clarke's anemonefish is the only species to occupy all nine, whereas other anemonefish favour a particular species. Introducing a familiar anemone usually results in host and fish uniting more quickly.*

▲ *The tomato anemonefish (Amphiprion frenatus) is another powerful species (females 14cm, males a little smaller) that is prepared to defend its host anemone vigorously. It does well with the bubbletip anemone (Entacmaea quadricolor).*

ANEMONEFISHES

▶ *Once settled, the instantly recognisable and hugely popular common clownfish (Amphiprion ocellaris) accepts a range of live and dried aquarium foods.*

* The common clownfish is one of the most popular fish raised in captivity. Given the availability of beautifully marked, healthy captive-bred specimens, it is hard to justify large-scale collection of this species from the wild.

Body colour is variable, ranging from pale yellow to red-orange.

◀ *Although very similar to A. ocellaris, the percula clownfish (A. percula) has more black pigment on the body.*

Many species of anemonefish can have incomplete vertical bands.

Its larger size (females up to 17cm), deep coloration and three white stripes make the maroon anemonefish easy to identify.

▶ *Do not keep the maroon anemonefish (Premnas biaculeatus) with other anemonefish. It will dominate an aquarium, particularly when living with a host anemone. In the wild it exclusively inhabits the bubbletip anemone, but in the aquarium it can often fend for itself without an anemone.*

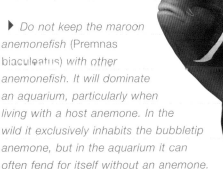

Damsels and Cardinals

Damselfishes are closely related to anemonefishes. While generally easy to care for, they may squabble amongst themselves, so provide an aquarium large enough to give each fish a reasonable amount of territory. Cardinalfishes are much less active than damsels or anemonefishes and may even be nocturnal. Juvenile cardinals of many species live close to or in anemones, but also use other invertebrates, such as sea urchins, for protection.

◀ *The undemanding blue-green chromis (Chromis viridis) is a small, shoaling damselfish, so keep it in a group of three or more. It will breed in the aquarium, where males dominate harems of females and vigorously guard the nest site.*

Males grow to a maximum size of 8cm, females are smaller.

▶ *It is often possible to house a group of Fijian blue-and-gold damselfishes (Chrysiptera taupou) in the aquarium, as long as the fish are stocked simultaneously and at a small size.*

▼ *Keep the Andaman damselfish (Pomacentrus alleni) with peaceful species that will not constantly chase it. It is not as robust as other damsels and if stressed, will not leave the refuge of the rockwork.*

The male fish has a black edge to the front part of the dorsal fin. In females, this region is yellow.

* The Andaman damselfish can turn its incredible colour and patterning on and off at will. This appears to be the result of a pecking order, whereby dominant individuals earn the right to display their full beauty.

◀ *The striking Banggai cardinalfish is one of the easiest marine fish to breed and raise in captivity. Try to obtain male/female pairs, otherwise fighting can occur. The fish can be kept in shoals in a sufficiently large aquarium.*

Mature males have a more massive jaw structure.

BREEDING THE BANGGAI

Once the female has deposited eggs in the form of a cluster or ball, they are taken into the mouth of the male for incubation. Even after hatching, the juvenile fishes remain in the mouth for protection from predators. When they emerge – as tiny, fully formed replicas of the adults – juveniles immediately seek out the protection of the long-spined sea urchin (Diadema *sp.*), with which they associate in the wild. It is not essential to keep sea urchins in order to rear this species successfully, but if they are not available, separate the juveniles from the adults, at least until they have grown larger. Some aquarists use artificial urchins with good results. Juvenile Banggai cardinals will sometimes protect themselves in anemones if urchins are not present in the aquarium. Feed the young as described on pages 54-55.

* During much of the day, the pyjama cardinalfish hides amongst the branches of stony corals. It becomes much more active at night or under blue actinic lights.

▶ *The benign behaviour and attractive coloration of the pyjama cardinalfish (Sphaeramia nematoptera) make it a popular choice with marine aquarists.*

The body is quite stocky and deep. Males are generally larger and have a larger mouth.

DAMSELS AND CARDINALS

Dwarf angelfishes

Most dwarf angelfishes (genus *Centropyge*) remain fairly small (less than 15cm). They are attractive, colourful and active, and a favourite of aquarists, particularly those with reef aquariums, even though they can never be fully trusted not to nip at invertebrates.

Good specimens appear bright-eyed and have a uniform blue body colour.

◀ *The cherub, or pygmy, angelfish (Centropyge argi) is the smallest of the dwarf angels; males measure 8cm, females 6cm.*

▶ *Bicolour dwarf angelfish (Centropyge bicolor) can be quite shy at first, hiding in the rockwork, but become bolder with time.*

Stunning coloration is a major feature. An emaciated fish with slightly faded colours may signify a weak or ailing specimen.

SEXING ANGELFISHES

All angelfishes are protogynous hermaphrodites, meaning that individuals are female first, becoming males as they grow larger. Determining sex is therefore difficult, except to say that the largest specimens will be males.

* The natural diet of the bicolour angelfish consists of sponges, tunicates, algae, small worms and crustaceans. Reproduce this variety in the aquarium and offer dried algae on which the fish can browse. Add vitamin supplements to frozen formula foods, mysis and brineshrimp. In time, fish should take flake or granular food.

◀ *The coral beauty (Centropyge bispinosa) is one of the most commonly kept marine fish, famed for its beauty and hardiness.*

Specimens have varying patterns depending on where they were collected.

* Centropyge dwarf angelfish can be mixed in the aquarium – with care. The coral beauty is the most relaxed and therefore least territorial, so if you are considering including this species, plus another couple of dwarf angels, put the coral beauty in first to minimise any conflict.

▲ *The flame dwarf angelfish (Centropyge loricula) is an instantly recognisable, highly desirable, but expensive addition to the marine aquarium. Offer it plenty of grazing material and some of the formula foods designed for dwarf angelfishes, plus mysis, brineshrimp and other meaty foods.*

Keep in a well-established system (more than 12 months old) stocked with plenty of live rock.

▲ *Specimen selection and a varied diet are the keys to long-term success with the small, peaceful, but timid multibanded dwarf angelfish (Centropyge multifasciata).*

OTHER POPULAR CENTROPYGE SPECIES

C. aurantia Golden angel
C. eibli Red stripe dwarf angel
C. flavissimus Lemonpeel dwarf angel
C. ferrugatus Rusty dwarf angel
C. heraldi Herald's angel
C. multicolor Multicolour dwarf angel
C. potteri Potter's dwarf angel

DWARF ANGELFISHES

True angelfishes

True angelfishes (family Pomacanthidae) include the genera *Pomacanthus, Apolemichthys, Chaetodontoplus, Pygoplites* and *Holacanthus*, all medium to large fish, often with personalities to match. They are often available as small juveniles, some with a markedly different appearance to the adult. Given sufficiently good water quality, most settle well into the aquarium, but do not be tempted by beautiful juveniles if you cannot house a large specimen long term.

◀ *Although not the most colourful angelfish, the cream angel (Apolemichthys xanthurus) is one of the cheapest to buy and easy to maintain in captivity.*

Ensure that a specimen has clear eyes and is feeding well before you buy it.

▼ *The stunning appearance of the adult emperor angelfish (Pomacanthus imperator) makes it an aquarium favourite – but it is an expensive fish to buy.*

▼ *The juvenile is equally attractive, but does not resemble the adult in any way. Fish undergoing the transition from juvenile to adult are not particularly appealing.*

* Specialist foods for angelfishes are important, but the cream angelfish is also known to take dried algae, mysis, brineshrimp and chopped shellfish. Given time and a patient aquarist, it may even accept flake and granular foods.

Juveniles are recognised as cleaner fish and therefore not harmed by much larger species.

▼ *Its generally trustworthy behaviour and relatively small maximum size (males 28cm, females smaller), make the majestic angelfish* (Pomacanthus navarchus) *the most popular* Pomacanthus *species to be maintained in the reef aquarium.*

ADULT COLORATION

Both *Pomacanthus navarchus* and *P. xanthometapon* (the blueface angel) can undergo metamorphosis to the adult coloration when very small. Fully transformed adults measuring 6cm or so are not uncommon and often settle better than larger individuals.

The majestic angelfish lives close to or in rockwork. It is prepared to hide for long periods to avoid the attentions of territorial fish.

Males and females both grow to 25cm.

▶ *The regal angelfish* (Pygoplites diacanthus) *is often the target of bullying by larger tangs and other angels, so does best when kept as the largest fish in a peaceful aquarium.*

* In the wild, the regal angelfish feeds on sponges. Provide preparations designed for such species, plus frozen foods, vitamin supplements and nori (a seaweed substitute). In time, they may take dried and flake foods.

Red Sea and Indian Ocean specimens have a yellow pelvic region and these should be the only individuals attempted by marine aquarists.

Butterflyfishes

The majority of butterflyfishes available in the aquarium hobby are members of a single genus, *Chaetodon*, and have a very similar body pattern. Notable exceptions are the genera *Chelmon, Forcipiger* and *Heniochus*, but all require similar care in the home aquarium. Feeding is the major challenge; be sure to investigate the long-term dietary requirements of any species you propose to buy. Those that include zooplankton as part of their natural diet are some of the easiest to maintain.

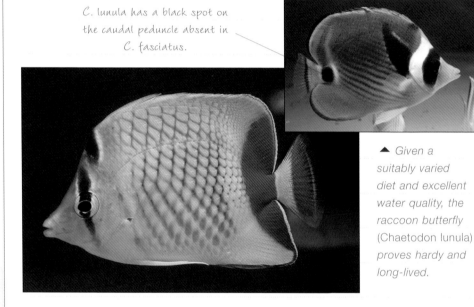

C. lunula has a black spot on the caudal peduncle absent in C. fasciatus.

▲ *Given a suitably varied diet and excellent water quality, the raccoon butterfly (Chaetodon lunula) proves hardy and long-lived.*

▲ *The Pacific pearlscale (Chaetodon xanthurus) is beautiful and inexpensive. It is one of a group of butterflyfish in which a sector of the rear of the dorsal fin and body is coloured orange. Fortunately, all require similar care.*

* The Red Sea raccoon (Chaetodon fasciatus) requires similar care to C. lunula, but is more expensive due to its collection area.

OTHER POPULAR CHAETODON SPECIES

C. argentatus Black pearlscale butterfly
C. auriga Threadfin butterfly
C. burgessi Burgess's butterfly
C. collare Collared butterfly
C. kleini Sunburst butterfly
C. miliaris Milletseed butterflyfish
C. punctatofasciatus Spotband butterfly
C. semilarvatus Masked butterflyfish
C. striatus Banded butterflyfish

▶ *Selecting a fish that is feeding well in the dealer's tank and then offering it a good diet are the keys to success when keeping the copperband butterflyfish (Chelmon rostratus). Provide a variety of frozen foods, including shellfish and particularly mysis shrimp, which have a higher fat content than brineshrimp. Feed several times a day and supplement the diet regularly with vitamins.*

* *Do not be tempted to introduce the copperband butterflyfish to control the pest anemone species Aiptasia, without giving due consideration to the fish's long-term requirements.*

A peaceful species that becomes increasingly confident as it settles into the aquarium.

Given plenty of attention, the copperband can prove hardy and long-lived.

◀ *The very long, slender snout of the longnosed butterflyfish (Forcipiger flavissimus) enables the fish to remove invertebrates from deep crevices. In the aquarium it accepts most foods, especially mysis and brineshrimp.*

* *If threatened by large surgeonfishes and tangs, the longnosed butterflyfish will 'headstand', exposing erect dorsal spines in the direction of the threat.*

POSSIBLE CONFUSION

Distinguishing between *Forcipiger flavissimus* and the only other species in the genus, *F. longirostris*, is difficult unless you have two specimens side by side. Look for scales with a dark-pigmented centre on the thorax of *F. longirostris*.

Wrasses

There are many species of wrasse available, ranging from the large and belligerent to the very small and reclusive. Many hogfishes and wrasses show widely varying temperaments between individuals of the same species. Many wrasses show markedly different coloration as they mature and some are sexually dimorphic (transforming from female to male). The term hogfish is generally applied to some of the large wrasse species, most of which grow too large for the home aquarium.

Males are larger and more brightly coloured. Females keep their less vivid juvenile coloration.

◀ *The stunningly coloured Maldive velvet fairy wrasse (Cirrhilabrus rubrisquamis) is one of several similar species with the same requirements. Keep it in a peaceful aquarium and offer enriched brineshrimp, mysis, chopped shellfish and dried algae. Vitamin supplements help to maintain the vibrant coloration.*

▼ *The female leopard wrasse (Macropharyngodon meleagris) has the leopard markings, while the larger male has orange and green bands on the head, giving way to a deep rusty red body with turquoise spots. This shy species does best in a mature aquarium stocked with plenty of live rock.*

✳ In common with other species in this group, the Maldive velvet fairy wrasse will sometimes jump out of an uncovered aquarium.

WRASSES

◀ The pyjama wrasse (Pseudocheilinus hexataenia) can prove angelic or demonic, depending on the individual concerned! This small species (males up to 10cm, females and juveniles no more than 5cm) can be kept singly or in male/female pairs.

* Faded colours may indicate that a fish is stressed or has been held in the dealer's tank for some time. After a short period in a home aquarium, the colours become brilliant once more.

▲ The eightline wrasse (Pseudocheilinus octotaenia) may be less striking than its close relative Pseudocheilinus hexataenia) but grows larger (14cm maximum) and is very hardy in captivity.

▶ The adult coral hogfish (Bodianus mesothorax) looks markedly different to the juvenile, which is jet-black with bright yellow spots around the eyes and on the body. The change in coloration occurs quickly at sizes of 5-6cm. Small specimens in adult coloration tend to be hardier and less timid than juveniles.

Male and female coral hogfish grow to 25cm. They are sturdy fish with assertive personalities.

Tangs

Tangs from the genera *Zebrasoma* and *Ctenochaetus* are very popular aquarium fish, not only because they are beautiful, but also because they play a useful role in the control of nuisance algae. However, these herbivorous fish can be highly territorial and you must take care when introducing them into an aquarium where some of the more belligerent species are already present.

This subadult has lost the juvenile colours.

◀ *With males and females measuring 25cm, the chevron tang (Ctenochaetus hawaiiensis) is the largest species of bristletooth tang. In the wild the fish use their brushlike teeth to remove fine algal films and detritus from rock surfaces. They are perfectly suited to a reef system.*

The expensive chevron tang is most commonly available as a juvenile.

* Pale specimens may have been in the dealer's tank for some time. They are 'good buys', as they will be settled and well acclimatised.

▶ *The beautiful purple tang (Zebrasoma xanthurum) is available at very small sizes, but soon grows larger than Z. flavescens, reaching 25cm. In most situations, and regardless of the other species stocked, it will become the dominant fish in any aquarium.*

◀ The hugely popular yellow sailfin tang (Zebrasoma flavescens) *achieves a moderate maximum size (20cm) and does a useful job in preventing unwanted algae.*

A SUITABLE DIET

Wild yellow sailfin tangs feed on filamentous algae, bul graze many different forms of algae in the home aquarium, including some *Caulerpa* and *Sargassum* species. Where there is no algae present, provide dried forms. (Lettuce is a poor substitute for natural marine algae.) Supplement the algae with mysis, brineshrimp, flaked and pellet foods.

This tang is one of the most commonly kept marine species. It is the principal marine fish export from Hawaii.

The behaviour of this species can change from quite submissive when small to belligerent when large.

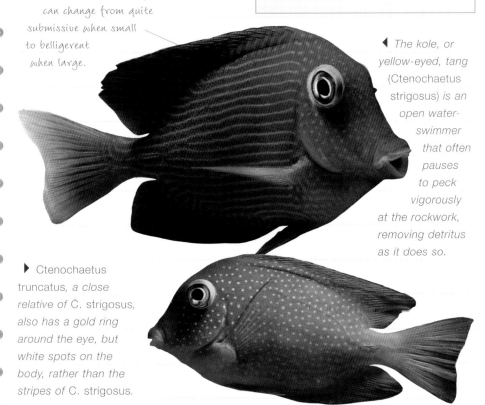

◀ The kole, or yellow-eyed, tang (Ctenochaetus strigosus) *is an open water-swimmer that often pauses to peck vigorously at the rockwork, removing detritus as it does so.*

▶ Ctenochaetus truncatus, *a close relative of* Ċ. strigosus, *also has a gold ring around the eye, but white spots on the body, rather than the stripes of* C. strigosus.

TANGS

Surgeonfishes

Surgeonfishes possess a pair of modified scales on the caudal peduncle that are scalpel-sharp, hence the name 'surgeonfish'. These can be used in attack or defence and are capable of inflicting painful wounds to both aquarists and fish. Members of the genus *Acanthurus* are notoriously territorial, but provided you allow for their growth and are sensible with subsequent stocking, you can enjoy a surgeonfish without having to endure their territorial aggression.

▲ *The 'scalpel' near the junction of the tail and body shines white here as a warning to predators to keep away.*

The adult coloration is uniformly blue. Juveniles are bright yellow.

▶ *The Atlantic blue surgeonfish (Acanthurus coeruleus) can be highly territorial, severely harassing newly introduced fish. Keep it in a large system (400 litres or more) and make this fish one of the final larger fish introduced into any aquarium.*

A. pyroferus has more attractive adult coloration than A. tristis (the Indian Ocean mimic surgeonfish).

◀ *If you like the shape and activity of the surgeonfish, but cannot stock a fish with aggressive tendencies, the Pacific Ocean mimic surgeonfish (Acanthurus pyroferus) is ideal. In the wild, juveniles mimic two, possibly three, angelfish species.*

* Large individuals are capable of moving unsecured pieces of rockwork or coral base rock as they browse on the algae growing there.

Look for signs of weight loss, which is common in underfed specimens of this active species.

▼ Despite its size (males and females 45cm) and well-developed caudal spines, the orangespine unicornfish (Naso lituratus) is not well able to defend itself against more aggressive species, such as large Acanthurus surgeonfishes. It will cohabit with them, but introduce it first to minimise potential problems.

Regal tangs are lively and active unless stressed or threatened, in which case they wedge themselves into any available crevice.

* The regal tang is prone to contracting protozoan parasite infestations shortly after introduction. Offering foods soaked in garlic can help to prevent an outbreak.

▲ The regal tang (Paracanthurus hepatus) is one of the most popular marine fish due to its striking coloration and availability. To house it long term, keep it in a 500-litre plus aquarium. Small specimens soon outgrow a small system.

Triggers and Puffers

Triggerfishes are named for the short, curved dorsal spine that can be used to anchor the fish into rocky crevices from which they cannot be removed unless they intentionally release their locking mechanism. Research the dietary requirements and temperament of any species you propose buying and do not acquire it unless you have a system capable of holding it in the long term. Species that feed largely on zooplankton in the wild tend to be less aggressive or destructive in the aquarium.

▲ *The clown triggerfish* (Balistoides conspicillum) *is a gorgeous, long-lived and highly entertaining marine fish – but be aware that it grows rapidly to 45cm and will become quite aggressive – even potentially lethal – towards its tankmates.*

The Picasso triggerfish is named for its delicate pigment markings.

▲ *The Picasso triggerfish* (Rhinecanthus aculeatus) *grows to 30cm and needs a large aquarium, a variety of meaty foods, including 'shell-on' molluscs and crustaceans, and hardy tankmates.*

▼ *Given its natural zooplankton-feeding instincts, the blue throat trigger* (Xanthichthys auromarginatus) *is arguably the triggerfish species most suited for introduction into a reef aquarium.*

Only the male has the blue throat patch and yellow margins to the anal, dorsal and tail fins.

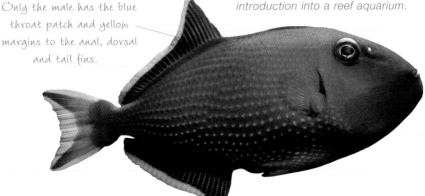

As a defence mechanism, pufferfishes and porcupinefishes are able to inflate their bodies by sucking in water, which makes them appear larger and more intimidating. In captivity, inflation is only seen in response to an imminent threat or severe stress. *Diodon* species are covered with spines that become erect when they inflate, while other species have skin or internal organs that are toxic.

This pufferfish can be maintained with many other types of fishes with few problems, but is not reef-safe.

▶ *The blackspotted pufferfish* (Arothron nigropunctatus) *is hardy and long-lived and will become quite tame. Provide this omnivore with a varied diet, including dried algae to satisfy its browsing instincts.*

▼ *Its entertaining behaviour and bizarre appearance make the porcupine pufferfish* (Diodon holocanthus) *a popular choice. Provide meaty foods, preferably in their shells, but bear in mind that this diet puts a heavy demand on the filtration system.*

* The porcupine pufferfish is nocturnal and may rest during the day, becoming more active at night. However, as aquarists usually 'train' it to receive food during the day, it often becomes more active at this time.

Males and females of this tempting species grow to 45cm.

Groupers and Grammas

Although most grouper species are large, predatory fish, they have close relatives that are quite easy to care for long term in the aquarium. Grammas are small, colourful elongate fish; both they and the dottybacks are found close to and amongst rockwork. All can be considered predators, so take care when selecting suitable tankmates, as smaller fish and invertebrates can fall victim to their carnivorous tendencies.

◀ *The comet grouper (Calloplesiops altivelis) has a secretive nature and remains hidden for prolonged periods.*

The golden forktail often swims upside-down

* The comet grouper is also known as the marine betta because its fins resemble those of the freshwater Siamese fighting fish, Betta splendens.

▲ *The golden forktail (Assessor flavissimus), a close relative of the comet grouper, is a peaceful, open-water swimmer and ideal for a reef aquarium.*

POTENTIALLY LARGE

The snowflake, or panther, grouper *(Chromileptes altivelis)* is widely available and instantly recognisable. However, it is a predator that grows slowly but steadily to a considerable size – males 70cm, females smaller. Attractive, hardy individuals are often on sale at 5-6cm long, but unless you have a large enough aquarium (minimum 900 litres) you will have problems later on.

▲ *Tank-bred snowflake groupers may command a higher price than wild fish, but bear in mind that this species is under great pressure in the wild from collectors and fishermen alike.*

* Do not confuse the royal gramma with the similarly coloured false gramma, or royal dottyback (Pseudochromis paccagnellae), an aggressive species from the Western Pacific.

▲ *The stunningly coloured and easy-to-keep royal gramma (Gramma loreto) will thrive in almost any system that does not house more aggressive fish.*

The tiny sunrise dottyback (males 7.5cm, females 6.5cm), accepts most small meaty food particles, including brineshrimp, mysis and chopped shellfish.

▲ *The small but beautifully coloured orchid dottyback (Pseudochromis fridmani), settles well into the aquarium. Pairs spawn frequently. Males guard the eggs laid in caves and may disappear from view at this time.*

▲ *Given plenty of rocky cover, a pair of sunrise dottybacks (Pseudochromis flavivertex), will behave perfectly naturally in the home aquarium.*

PEACEFUL DOTTYBACKS

Red Sea and Arabian Gulf specimens of dottyback (*Pseudochromis* spp.) are often more peaceful than their Indo-Pacific counterparts. They include the orchid dottyback (*P. fridmani*), sunrise (*P. flavivertex*), neon-lined (*P. aldabraensis*) and Sankey's (*P. sankeyi*). The Red Sea species are often available as captive-bred individuals.

Blennies

There are many species of peaceful, small blennies to choose from. They can be roughly divided into herbivores and planktivores. Herbivores include *Ecsenius bicolor* (bicolour blenny) and *Salarius fasciatus* (jewelled rockskipper, or common algae blenny). Both species keep algae under control in the reef. Do not mix species of herbivorous blennies in the smaller aquarium as this can lead to fighting. Planktivores can be typified by *Ecsenius midas* (Midas blenny), an endearing, colourful species.

◀ *The bicolour blenny* (Ecsenius bicolor) *swims actively in the water column in pursuit of food and then reverses back into its retreat to survey its surroundings from a safe vantage point.*

▶ *The beautiful Red Sea mimic blenny* (Ecsenius gravieri) *mimics the blue-headed canary blenny* (Meiacanthus nigrolineatus), *which has venomous fangs. However, the mimic is harmless and hardy, peaceful and full of character.*

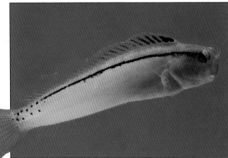

FANG BLENNIES

The genus *Meiacanthus* contains a number of species known as 'fang blennies' on account of the very large canine teeth, with a venom gland at their base, found on the lower jaw. The Indo-Pacific *M. atrodorsalis* is mimicked by a yellow and blue form of *Ecsenius bicolor*.

* In the absence of the mimicked species, Ecsenius gravieri will remain almost exclusively on the rockwork. It is not necessary to maintain the two species together.

MIDAS BLENNY

The fascinating Midas blenny *(Ecsenius midas)* mimics the lyretail anthias *(Pseudanthias squamipinnis)*, swimming into open water with them and feeding on zooplankton. *E. midas* has separate colour forms that are visible when it is resting, but these change when it is shoaling with the anthias. The Indonesian form of Midas blenny is the most variable in colour, ranging from yellow-orange to green-brown.

▼ *The Midas blenny* (Ecsenius midas) *is often found in association with shoaling wreckfish* (Pseudanthias spp.). *It alternates an open-water, highly active swimming style with prolonged periods of rest on the rockwork.*

A DUAL PERSONALITY

If the algae blenny is confronted by a larger, more dominant fish in its territory, it may act shyly, but once that fish retreats, the algae blenny then bullies a fish smaller than itself. Its aggression is more apparent in a small aquarium.

▼ *The algae blenny* (Salarius fasciatus) *is popular with many aquarists on account of its interesting behaviour and because it consumes certain forms of filamentous algae and detritus. Given its large adult size (males 14cm, females a little smaller), it will require a suitably sized aquarium (at least 250 litres).*

Provide dried algae on a daily basis for the best results with this blenny. Many specimens will accept mysis and brineshrimp, amongst other meaty foods.

Gobies

Gobies tend to have large heads and mouths and cylindrical bodies. They often have a sucker on their underside, formed from the fusion of the pelvic fins, that enables them to perch on vertical surfaces. Many species form commensal relationships with shrimps of the genus *Alpheus* and make a fascinating feature in any aquarium.

DIMINUTIVE AND POPULAR

At just 5cm, female blue neon gobies are a little larger than males. Females are capable of changing sex, so if you intend keeping more than one individual, buy small specimens or try selecting two fish with a significant size difference. This species has been successfully bred in captivity.

▲ *The blue neon goby* (Elacatinus oceanops) *is a tiny cleaner fish that uses the fused pelvic fins to hold onto the fish it is cleaning. It then hops over the surface of the fish's body in search of dead skin or foreign bodies.*

* The goby family is the largest group of marine fish, numbering over 2000 species.

The yellow prawn goby's coloration is highly variable, ranging from brilliant yellow to grey and even brown forms or combinations of each colouring.

▲ *The yellow prawn goby* (Cryptocentrus cinctus) *is the most widely available of all the gobies known to live in the burrows made by pistol shrimps (genus* Alpheus*).*

▶ *The dragon goby* (Amblygobius phalaena) *is a medium-large species (males and females 15cm) that makes an interesting alternative to gobies from the genus* Valenciennea. *It shares their sand-sifting behaviour, but is less prone to weight loss in the aquarium.*

This female dragon goby has a single spot on the tail fin. Males have a number of spots.

* Many species of goby use their mouths to separate morsels of food from inedible sand, which they then expel through the gills. Species from the genus Valenciennea need several feeds a day of high-energy mysis shrimp or chopped shellfish to satisfy their nutritional needs.

Males and females grow to 6cm. They have a large mouth that gapes when the fish is threatened.

THE GOBY AND THE SHRIMP

The shrimp digs a burrow and the goby stands guard over the entrance. Should danger threaten, both retreat quickly into the tunnel. Industrious shrimp can create a network of interconnected chambers, so be sure to secure the rockwork firmly.

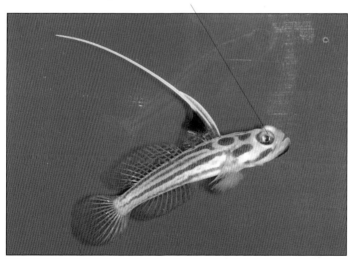

◀ *The stunning white-rayed shrimp goby* (Stonogobiops yasha) *is becoming easier to obtain, but remains expensive. It forms a symbiotic relationship with the alpheid pistol shrimp* Alpheus randalli. *In the absence of a shrimp, the fish may not feed.*

GOBIES

Cowfishes and Boxfishes

Cowfishes and boxfishes are very similar groups, characterised by species in which the skeleton has become fused into a rigid structure containing all the internal organs. Cowfishes tend to enhance this protection with long spines, and both cowfishes and boxfishes secrete noxious venom from their skin. Nevertheless, they should not be housed with aggressive species. Do not be tempted by tiny individuals, which cannot deal very well with high water flow and need plenty of specialised attention to thrive.

▶ *When stressed or threatened, the longhorn cowfish (Lactoria cornuta) can exude a toxin that is lethal to all the aquarium inhabitants, including itself. In the wild it would swim away from the danger, but this is not possible in the confines of an aquarium. House this peaceful species with equally tolerant tankmates.*

The body becomes more elongate with age, reaching 46cm, even in the aquarium.

An alert specimen will feed well and often 'follows' people as they pass the tank.

▲ *The longhorn cowfish's common name refers to the paired, hornlike projections over each eye, one pointing forwards and one to the rear. The pectoral fins are used for propulsion and the tail as a rudder.*

FEEDING THE COWFISH

The longhorn cowfish is a specialised feeder that blows jets of water from its mouth to expose food items in the sandy substrate. These may include small burrowing molluscs, worms and crustaceans. Although it may attempt this behaviour in the aquarium, it will also accept food from the water column. Offer dried algae, mysis, brineshrimp, enriched formula food and vitamin supplements.

◀ *The yellow boxfish* (Ostracion cubicus) *is both beautiful and popular, but not easy to maintain in the aquarium. Feed it at least three times per day on meaty foods or an enriched formula diet. Provide continual access to dried algae.*

Adult yellow boxfishes will dominate other fish in the tank. Provide robust tankmates that will not bother the boxfish.

Young specimens resemble little yellow dice, but their colours may fade in time.

◀ *Boxfishes are often available as inexpensive, small juveniles, but can be bullied by aggressive fish of any size. The defensive toxin they emit can prove lethal. Juveniles need plenty of hiding places.*

The male black boxfish is larger and more extravagantly patterned than the female.

▲ *The beautiful black boxfish* (Ostracion meleagris) *requires more care than most other commonly available species. This is another species that can emit a lethal toxin if stressed or threatened.*

BOXFISH PAIRS

Ostracion meleagris is one of the few boxfish species available in male/ female pairs. Males (which grow up to 25cm) are more costly than female specimens (less than 15cm), but true pairs are expensive.

Miscellaneous species

Fishes kept within the marine fish hobby include a number of species not closely related to each other or those described elsewhere in this book. They include the dartfishes, which swim actively in the water column, the substrate-dwelling dragonets, the predatory lionfishes and the fascinating pipefishes.

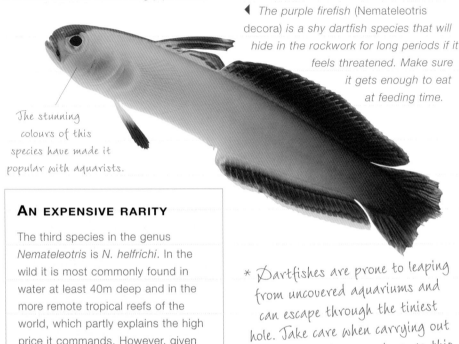

◀ *The purple firefish* (Nemateleotris decora) *is a shy dartfish species that will hide in the rockwork for long periods if it feels threatened. Make sure it gets enough to eat at feeding time.*

The stunning colours of this species have made it popular with aquarists.

AN EXPENSIVE RARITY

The third species in the genus *Nemateleotris* is *N. helfrichi*. In the wild it is most commonly found in water at least 40m deep and in the more remote tropical reefs of the world, which partly explains the high price it commands. However, given the right care it will prove a hardy and long-lived aquarium specimen.

* Dartfishes are prone to leaping from uncovered aquariums and can escape through the tiniest hole. Take care when carrying out any work in the aquarium, as this can be stressful enough for the fish to begin leaping.

▶ *Flame firefishes* (Nemateleotris magnifica) *are best kept in male/female pairs. Housed with non-aggressive tankmates and fed on finely chopped shellfish, brineshrimp and mysis, they should prove hardy in the aquarium.*

Despite its common name, this fish grows to about 17cm and may consume small tankmates.

▲ *The fuzzy dwarf lionfish (Dendrochirus brachypterus) is one of the commonest species of venomous fish known as turkey- or lionfish, and easy to keep in captivity. Small individuals (3-4cm) accept frozen brineshrimp and mysis. To encourage larger specimens to feed you may need to wriggle small whole fish in the water.*

* Take care when moving rockwork or cleaning the aquarium as this fish perches upside-down under ledges during the day. Lionfishes and scorpionfishes are venomous and can inflict painful injuries.

The clearfin becomes more active at feeding time or under blue actinic light.

SIZE CONSIDERATIONS

The Fumanchu *(Dendrochirus biocellatus)* is another reasonably sized lionfish for the aquarium, reaching about 13cm. Compare this with the commonly imported turkeyfish *(Pterois volitans)* which can reach a length of 50cm, quickly outgrowing a small aquarium and viewing smaller tankmates as food.

▲ *The clearfin, or 'radiata', lionfish (Pterois radiata) grows to about 10cm in captivity. Try to choose a specimen that is feeding on dead food; it is possible to acclimatise newly imported specimens to frozen foods over time, but it is best to acquire one that already accepts these.*

MISCELLANEOUS SPECIES

Miscellaneous species

Although commonly referred to as scooters, or scooter blennies, these highly popular fish are not blennies (Family Blennidae) but rather species of dragonet. The courtship of many dragonets can be observed in home marine aquariums and they will often spawn.

◀ *The pink scooter dragonet, or 'blenny', (Synchiropus ocellatus) will thrive where there is plenty of live rock harbouring natural populations of the copepods and amphipods that it loves to eat. It will also pick frozen foods such as brineshrimp from sandy substrates.*

Scooter blennies are highly variable in colour, ranging from almost brown to bright pink and red.

▶ *The male spotted mandarin dragonet (Synchiropus picturatus) is fiercely aggressive towards other males, but male/female pairs engage in fascinating courtship and spawning displays, which can take place regularly in most aquariums.*

◀ *In common with other* Synchiropus *species, the psychedelic mandarin dragonet* (Synchiropus splendidus) *relies on the presence of live rock to encourage the existence of small, self-sustaining populations of its natural food. Introducing similar species may mean they out-compete each other for the available food.*

This is a peaceful species when kept in pairs; two males will fight.

▲ *The blue-and-orange cleaner pipefish (Doryrhamphus excisus) is fairly easy to keep in captivity. Offer it frozen brineshrimp and mysis, but make sure the food is small enough for the fish's tiny mouth. This pipefish acts as a cleaner fish, removing parasites from larger fish. Do not house it with predatory species.*

BREEDING BEHAVIOUR

Male cleaner pipefish have bumps or notches on the snout, while the female's snout is smooth. Females deposit eggs in a brooding pouch located at the base of the tail on the underside of the male fish. The eggs are supplied with oxygen by the rich blood supply of the pouch lining. The larvae are difficult to rear.

SEAHORSES

Seahorses generally require high water quality and plenty of food. Since they are currently the subject of CITES restrictions, the vast majority of specimens on sale will be tank-raised. These should be feeding on frozen food, which makes it much easier to keep them. Live foods can be difficult to obtain in sufficient quantities year-round. A species aquarium housing several individuals suits them best, with a lack of strong water flow and plenty of holdfasts in the form of artificial corals, algae or gorgonians.

▶ *The yellow seahorse (Hippocampus kuda) grows to 25cm. Mature males have a breeding pouch into which the female deposits her eggs. While raising this species is not difficult, it does require a certain amount of dedication and can be time-consuming.*

Invertebrates

A modern marine aquarium is capable of providing excellent accommodation for a wide variety of invertebrates, including corals. This section looks at a small sample of some of the most commonly available species. Be sure to obtain accurate information about the species that interest you before you buy them.

▲ *Blue tubular sponges are difficult to maintain unless your aquarium is capable of meeting their requirements exactly.*

▲ *The red and blue forms of the popular Actinodiscus sp. mushroom anemone are hardy and easy to keep.*

▲ *Mushrooms, such as this* Rhodactis *sp., are hardy and undemanding. They tolerate slow water currents and spread readily.*

▶ *Although not easy to maintain, the bubble anemone (*Entacmaea quadricolor*) is one of the hardier host anemones.*

INVERTEBRATES

◀ *Giant button polyps* (Palythoa grandis) *are mostly available in shades of green and brown. This coral is undemanding but does best under strong lighting.*

▶ *Bush corals photosynthesise, but will do best when fed. They can grow very large in the home aquarium.*

▶ *The ever-popular* Lobophytum *leather corals are easy to maintain, but can secrete certain chemicals that inhibit the growth of their tankmates.*

▼ *Toadstool leather corals* Sarcophyton sp. *vary in the length and colour of their polyps. Provide strong illumination.*

▲ *Branching soft corals, such as* Cladiella sp. *can grow very large, very quickly. Give them plenty of room in the aquarium.*

Invertebrates

▲ Large polyp stony (LPS) corals are generally easier to maintain than small polyp stony (SPS) corals. This is a spiny brain coral, Lobophyllia sp.

▼ Hammer coral is a member of the genus Euphyllia, named for the unique shape of its polyps.

STINGING CORALS

Coral reefs are tough places to eek out an existence, especially if you are rooted to the spot like many corals. Many species have strong defences in the form of specialised cells that are capable of inflicting painful stings. Euphyllia species can sting rival corals from a distance. Take care around such corals and wash your hands if you come into contact with them.

◀ The tentacles of the cornet coral (Euphyllia glabrescens) are capable of stinging their neighbours, so give this species plenty of room for expansion and growth.

▶ *Tube, fan or featherduster worms, such as this* Sabellastarte *species, are inexpensive and commonly available. Tubeworms and corals differ in that corals derive much of their food from symbiotic algae. These are contained in their tissues and utilise the strong lighting available in the reef aquarium to synthesise sugars. Tubeworms, however, must obtain their nourishment from fine particles in the water column. There are several commercially available kinds of 'invertebrate diet' for these animals.*

◀ *Herbivorous snails from the genus* Trochus *can grow large in the aquarium, but are invaluable in the control and prevention of unwanted forms of algae. It is often useful to add a few species of herbivorous snail to the aquarium, as each often shows preferences for different forms of alga.* Astraea *and* Turbo *snails are particularly good additions.*

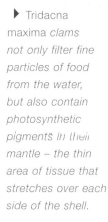

▶ Tridacna maxima *clams not only filter fine particles of food from the water, but also contain photosynthetic pigments in their mantle – the thin area of tissue that stretches over each side of the shell.*

Invertebrates

◀ *Skunk cleaner shrimps* (Lysmata amboinensis) *scavenge uneaten food intended for their vertebrate tankmates.*

▼ L. debelius *is less likely to stray into the open than* L. amboinensis, *but gains confidence with time.*

CHOOSE THE RIGHT SHRIMP

Beware of being wrongly sold candy, or dancing, shrimps *(Rhynchocinetes durbanensis)* as peppermint shrimps. These are not reef-friendly and eat polyps. *R. durbanensis* has a red body with prominent white stripes, absent in *L. wurdemanni*.

◀ *Peppermint shrimp* (L. wurdemanni) *can serve a useful role by consuming the pest anemone species* Aiptasia.

◀ *The blue-knuckled hermit crab (Calcinus elegans) is a dwarf species that seldom proves problematic to keep in the aquarium.*

* Provide spare shells of varying sizes for all hermit crabs. Without them, fighting may ensue over suitable shells.

▲ *The scarlet hermit crab, or 'red-legged hermit', is very useful at preventing unwanted algae.*

▲ Neopetrolisthes *spp.* anemone crabs prefer to live in stinging anemones. They trap food particles using netlike feeding appendages.

▶ *Many shrimps from the genus* Alpheus *share their burrows with gobies.*

INVERTEBRATES

Invertebrates

▶ *Small serpent starfish, such as this* Ophiolepis *sp., make excellent scavengers. Large species or individuals can predate fish and crustaceans.*

◀ *Species of serpent starfish range in colour from dull brown or black to brilliant crimson.*

▼ *Handle long-spined sea urchins (Diadema spp.) with care. They grow quite large and are not suitable for the smaller aquarium.*

Many sea urchins need lots of calcium to grow, often at the expense of calcareous algae.

CLOSE RELATIVES

Urchins, starfish and sea cucumbers are all echinoderms and therefore closely related, despite their very different appearances. Tunicates, or sea squirts, are distant relatives of all vertebrates, despite the resemblance of many species to simple sponges.

INVERTEBRATES

* Despite its common name, the 'spineless' urchin has short dense spines.

▲ The spineless urchin (Mespilia globulus) is frequently found covered in debris of various sorts that serves as camouflage.

▼ Most tunicates, such as the giant Pacific tunicate, are filter-feeders that require ample food to survive in captivity.

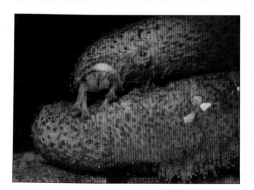

▲ The pink sea cucumber (Holothuria sp.) uses its short feeding tentacles to lift food particles from sandy substrates.

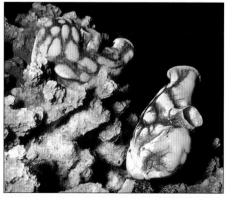

Picture credits

Additional picture credits

The publishers would like to thank the following photographers and companies for providing images, credited here by page number and position: T(Top), B(Bottom), C(Centre), BL(Bottom left), etc.

Aqua Medic: 13(TR)

Aqua Press (M-P & C. Piednoir) 72(C), 83(B)

Bioquatic Photo – A.J. Nilsen, (www. biophoto.net): 5(BL), 32(BL), 34(BR), 37(BL), 45(BL), 56(TL,CR), 76(CR), 86(TL), 87(T,B), 90(TL), 91(BR), 93(CL,BR), 94(T,CL), 95(T,BR)

D-D Aquarium Solutions: 13(CL)

GHL Products: 11(TL)

Tim Hayes: 54(TR)

Lisa Page: All pictures pages 38-41, 69(T), 92(BL)

Photomax (Max Gibbs): 51(BR), 72(B), 88(TL)

Iggy Tavares: 79(B), 80(T), 81(T)

Kevin Webb: 63(BL)